Christian Education
in a
Secular Society

W. R. NIBLETT

LONDON
OXFORD UNIVERSITY PRESS
NEW YORK TORONTO
1960

Oxford University Press, Amen House, London E.C.4

GLASGOW NEW YORK TORONTO MELBOURNE WELLINGTON
BOMBAY CALCUTTA MADRAS KARACHI KUALA LUMPUR
CAPE TOWN IBADAN NAIROBI ACCRA

Printed in Great Britain

PREFACE

In 1954 the Institute of Christian Education published a Report from its Study and Research Committee entitled *Religious Education in Schools* (S.P.C.K.). This was a carefully documented examination of the position and organization of religious education in schools in England and Wales. Since then the Committee has been reconstituted (see Appendix I) and given a new problem to tackle. The terms of reference which defined this problem were:

> To examine the practical tasks and objectives of Christian teachers in secondary schools in terms of their school situation, and in the wider contemporary social setting; and to consider how the Christian teacher can build up the attitude of pupils upon Christian foundations such as he himself accepts.

The outcome of our deliberations on this subject is this book—necessarily less factual in content than the Report of 1954, but not less surely founded on the evidence collected, of which we have considered a good deal given to us orally or submitted in the form of memoranda by teachers and others in many parts of the country (see Appendix II). We are grateful to them and also to the Schools Broadcasting Department of the B.B.C. for permitting us in Chapter Ten to draw upon an unpublished report from their own files. Though the book is the outcome of our consideration of this material together with our own thoughts at a series of meetings held over the past three years, it has been set down by one person, who made great use of written contributions from members of the Committee. Some members saw it in draft and made helpful criticisms and suggestions, but the responsibility for its composition, defects and errors is mine alone.

Leeds, 1959   W. R. NIBLETT

CONTENTS

INTRODUCTION

THIS BOOK sets forth some of the consequences of being a Christian teacher of adolescents in the present intellectual, moral and spiritual climate. It deals with possible ways in which a number of subjects in the school curriculum can prepare the ground for an education which is Christian. The book is addressed in the first instance to the many Christians on the staffs of schools; secondly to parents who are aware of some of the difficulties confronting boys and girls of twelve to eighteen today and who are concerned about the education their children are being given during their formative adolescent years; thirdly to thinking men and women generally who realize that there is an obvious relationship between the kind of education young people receive and the kind of country and world ours is to be in fifty years' time.

Tom, Dick and Mary are noticeably healthier, taller and heavier than was any generation of their predecessors. In general they are better housed, better fed, better clothed and better taught than children have ever been before. They stay at school for longer and statistics tell us that the proportion of children who take and pass external examinations (in a wider range of subjects than before) is steadily increasing. In addition they are acquiring during their schooldays a great variety of unexaminable techniques, skills and kinds of confidence. It has been suggested that they may not write as neatly or spell as accurately as did their parents at the same age, but the evidence is not altogether convincing. What is convincing, and encouraging, is that these children have learned more about science and crafts, are better informed on current events, have heard more music and taken part in more kinds of physical exercise, have travelled more widely on journeys organized by the schools themselves.

Their experience is broader; and they have more poise.

It might be thought indeed that education was improving so satisfactorily that there was little to be concerned about so long as peace is preserved and prosperity maintained. If peace is difficult to guarantee prosperity at least can be ensured, to some extent at any rate, by increased concentration on the teaching of science and technology.

But a deeper look may give us pause. What is the aim of the education we are giving? If education has anything to do with a committed way of life, if its concern is to include that level of living at all, the total picture may not be so rosy. Is it material benefits alone we are offering our children? To some parents this seems to be enough. 'I simply want my child to be happy at school: that's the main thing,' says Mrs. Smith. 'I want my boy to be just a normal boy,' says Mr. Jones. 'What they should be given,' say Mr. and Mrs. Robinson, 'is a fair chance of a job with good hours and good pay and a bit of respectability to it. That's what education is for.' Such attitudes reveal no sense that life may have a purpose greater than the welfare or happiness of the individual, or that it can imply commitment to an ideal, a way of life, a faith. Those who deny that life calls for such a commitment would of course emphatically deny also that home, school or university should have any concern for it. For throughout the English-speaking countries (as indeed in many others) there is a widespread assumption, even though unconsciously held, that it is material possessions that matter. They are after all the surest things in a world where uncertainties are so common, and where so many delights are possible for the healthy man who has the means to them.

And yet, in spite of the prevailing materialism of society, there is without any doubt a deep potential of interest among boys and girls in the great questions of the meaning and purpose of life, of faith and belief, of morality and conduct. There is a feeling among many young people—and it is shared by many adults—that life ought not merely to be, but to seem, more important than it now appears. Teddy-boyism and existentialism at their different levels are both protests against being simply 'carried along.' People need to *feel* they are alive as well as to be so, and if mere activity at its most violent is not enough to ensure this for more than a very limited time, at least it is better than doing nothing at all.

If brought to realize it many parents and many of their children might agree that their keen, almost unassuageable, desire for more comfort and success in the material sphere has a connexion with the uncertainty they feel about those great questions. They are uncertain not merely about the future of the world, but about the traditions of value within which our civilization has been nourished in the past, and about traditional Christianity itself. The 1944 Education Act, it is true, lays it down—and undoubtedly with the concurrence of the large majority of the people—that in every school the day should begin with a period of worship and that Religious Knowledge should regularly be taught. But this consent may for many parents be the heaving of a sigh of relief that they personally have now shifted some of their own responsibility in such matters to the nation. Let the school introduce boys and girls to religious knowledge and Christian values, since parents are no longer certain where they stand. One may suspect moreover that the widespread belief in science as a means to happiness is to many not only a genuine and conscious seizing of hope, but also, less consciously, an escape from the burden of spending mental energy in puzzling and worrying about long-term and major purposes in life. Here is a kind of short-term certainty, full of fascination and challenge.

Clearly there is a conflict of purposes and values in the minds both of parents and of boys and girls today, even if it is frequently unconscious and may show itself for a moment only to those who have the time and insight to recognize it. The conflict in the children may become only the more deeply repressed by the sort of education which a school today finds it easiest to give. Education in a sense of values, the nurture of belief, must not, by Christian teachers, be confined to the Scripture lesson and the morning assembly. If it is, the influence of these may be submerged under the many silent evaluations concealed in the overall teaching of the school, or within the teaching of particular subjects, each of which can have its own unconscious hierarchy of value-judgments. It is these which the Christian teacher will turn instead to good account.

CHAPTER ONE

Home and School

I

THE HOMES from which children come are deeply important to them in more than a physical sense. Most of what Sigrid Undset called 'the longest years' of a child's life are lived before his schooldays even begin. Home influence, in the 1960's as in the 1760's or the 1560's, is permeating and inward; for home is a place of close personal relationships, where the speech and standards and unconscious presuppositions of others are infectious. Nothing is more essential to an understanding of the educational process than a firm grip on the idea that very much education proceeds at an unconscious level, no one being aware that it is happening.

There is much evidence to show that a strong centre is given to a child's life if his parents believe firmly in certain values and pass those on to him, quite naturally and for the most part quite unconsciously. Such values might include, for example, the notion that it is 'done' to give oneself deeply in affection to someone else; that telling the truth is important and self-justified; that a loving God exists, can be prayed to, and is to be believed in. Those who develop such a centre have a strong defence against the pressures of external environment. There is, as it were, safety within this core for seeds of faith to grow.

For many reasons, however, there are fewer homes than there were which are good at nourishing cores; only a small proportion of children come from homes with the sure values common enough in peasants' and crofters' homes even fifty years ago. With the rapid change from an economy dominated by agriculture and the country to one dominated by industry and the town; with the wider awareness of other people's habits and different moral standards; and above all with the widespread decline in religious belief, has come a great uncertainty within the minds of many adults about the standards they can pass on with any deep conviction to their children.

Subtly encouraging them in these circumstances to trade out of the problem are three other influences. First, there is a general increase of self-consciousness so that people are more aware of their own doubts and of the questionable morality of teaching their children what they only half-believe themselves, however much they might wish that they had convictions. Secondly, there has been the teaching of many psychologists (heard because men were glad to hear it) that people could do much damage to children by trying to 'act as God' towards them or even to bias them to go in one direction rather than another. Far better, they taught, for parents to be as objective and 'uninvolved' as they could be in their teaching of religion and even morals. But, thirdly, and perhaps more far-reaching, there has been the general effect of living in a technological age with an abundance of material satisfactions at hand. During the last twenty-five years, poverty in this country has been greatly reduced; the numbers living below the poverty line have dropped from thirty per cent to around two per cent. There has been an enormous increase in the production of material goods, in a period in which the national population has risen by less than ten per cent, from forty-seven millions to fifty-one millions or so. At the same time, a really personal participation in the work they do is required only from a small proportion of men and women. All that is demanded for the most part, either from 'hands' or executives, is that they should use their particular skills or techniques and be patient; and results will come. One of the secrets for almost everybody lies indeed in not becoming too emotionally involved. Cool observation, detachment, non-identification, are marks of the scientific temper, and these are as necessary in the worker 'on the line' at a mass-production plant, as in his fellow-employee in the research laboratory or even in the personnel manager or highly placed administrator working for the same firm. The emphasis is upon harnessing and making use of nature and human nature; and upon coming to understand it just enough for that purpose.

In view of these and other factors it is undoubtedly more difficult to be fully committed to any one view of life, Christian or otherwise, than it used to be. You have to go down more deeply into yourself and wrestle if you are to discover what is greatest and deepest in you. In earlier times you could, even if you were very intelligent or self-conscious, be committed to traditional views and values without need for any searching self-examination. That is no longer possible; and it takes great energy and self-denial to find in detail what you really can believe in. It takes also a freedom from distraction which in a mid-twentieth century environment it is difficult to find. The fact is that to many in the mid-twentieth century positive and deeply held belief is apt to be regarded as an attribute of less civilized people. Non-involvement seems almost to be a part of safety, firm affirmation to have something of a toxic character.

A child now growing up in England will in very many cases go to school from a home which has relatively few definite beliefs and moral principles to pass on. But more significant still, in some ways, it may well be a home which offers comparatively little in range of experience and emphasizes safety and comfort overmuch. Suburban living tends to banish birth, death and severe pain to nursing homes, to keep eccentricity and enthusiasm out of sight and to cut off both grown-ups and children from many experiences basic to life in earlier periods. Daily living for more and more men and women—as new housing estates increase in number—is a fragmented affair. The rootlessness of life in the suburbs, where very many live already and where even more people will live in the future, is one of its most obvious features. Without any doubt families now inhabiting better types of houses are living a more self-contained and self-sufficient existence than they were twenty years ago, but probably a more self-centred one too. The family is a more isolated unit than it used to be.

It is easy to underestimate the extent to which children model themselves, consciously and unconsciously, to fit the expectations of their homes and their world. Margaret Mead's *Growing Up in New Guinea* provides abundant evidence of the extraordinary readiness of children to assume the attitudes and characteristics which adults expect. The physical skills and social prudery which the Manus parents really demanded of their children became ingrained habits; for the rest, it was the children who dominated the parents:

'The Manus' conception of social discipline is as loose as their standards of physical training are rigid. They demand nothing beyond physical efficiency and respect for property except a proper observance of the canons of shame. Children must learn privacy in excretion almost by the time they can walk; must get by heart the conventional attitudes of shame and embarrassment. This is communicated to them not by sternness and occasional chastisement, but through the emotions of their parents. The parents' horror, physical shrinking, and repugnance are communicated to the careless child. This adult attitude is so strong that it is as easy to impregnate the child with it as it is to communicate panic. . . . Into this atmosphere of prudery and shame the children are early initiated. They are wrapped about with this hot prickling cloak until the adults feel safe from embarrassing betrayal. And here social discipline ceases. The children are taught neither obedience nor deference to their parents' wishes. A two-year-old child is permitted to flout its mother's humble request that it come home with her. At night the children are supposed to be at home at dark, but this does not mean that they go home when called. Unless hunger drives them there the parents have to go about collecting them, often by force.'

After a passage like this it is interesting to examine the attitudes demanded of children during these mid-century years in our own country. Like the Manus we are taking a lot of trouble to make the young thoroughly familiar with some of the essential physical skills of a mechanised civilization. Kerb drill is taught with increasing efficiency. The rules of diet and exercise for a healthy physical life are more widely known and more extensively practised than ever before. Children can use their bodies in games and physical activities with a discipline and control that enable them to achieve very high standards of performance. What is less obvious is any comparable development in emotional awareness and response to human situations. There is a large measure of agreement about the skills of which we want them to be capable, but far less understanding of the persons that we want them to become, or the beliefs about God or the nature of things that we want them to have.

As soon as they were capable of being aware of anything the Manus children understood the social tabus of their tribe. These were not simply important; they were absolute. The world in which they were growing up was a world in which a few things mattered enormously; for the rest they could please themselves. This lack of concern for the whole of life made their social system loveless and arbitrary. The

things they cared about provided no co-ordinating link between their different experiences, and their way of life had
no centre of faith and confidence. The attitudes that the
childen developed were an inadequate basis for full personal
relationships when they grew up, because they were a reflection of a society itself deficient in personal relationships.

This evidence would suggest that the attitudes of children
in any society reflect so closely those of the adults that when
we draw attention to the attitudes which are desirable in
children we are in effect drawing attention to those which
we think desirable in ourselves. If the children are deficient
in some of the qualities that we could wish they possessed,
what we are looking at is a mirror reflecting our own
deficiencies.

A family life which has some richness about it is of enormous importance educationally. Such a life gives scope for
love and suffering and awe; for a natural learning within
the family circle of human differences sexual and tempera-
mental; and for the learning too of the underlying importance of a natural obedience by those within the family—
regardless of age and sex and temperament—to common
standards and principles. A family life which gives such
things is not the prerogative of any one social class : it is as
possible in a poor home as in a wealthy one. Adults in
general today see the dangers of commitment far more
clearly than they see the dangers of non-commitment. Nor
is the possible connection realized between an emotionally
'thin' childhood home and that unwillingness to become
involved which is so marked a feature of mid-twentieth
century life.

If a child has no core of loves and beliefs which is firm
he is likely to be very much more subject to passing fashion;
he will be 'other directed' by his contemporaries and by
advertisements. 'It doesn't pay to care.' He may well substi-

tute a belief in fate, luck, chance, for others less superficial; or concentrate on work for an entirely material kind of prosperity. A child who sees no harm in stealing a car for the sake of a spree, or expressing his 'individuality' here, there and everywhere—i.e. a child who is delinquent—is an extreme example of a child who is not ballasted or committed, who has no core. Today in western Europe many boys and girls are being convicted of delinquency. It may well be that more people are 'near-delinquent' now than in a more stable and committed time. Certainly Teddy-boyism is not symptomatic of any deep emotional involvement in life but rather the opposite. It is an attempt to give life a point and purpose it otherwise lacks.

II

If we look with penetration at the real education being given to our children in their schools, among the questions we should ask are such as these: What are the presuppositions and ideals being fed into their unconscious minds not only by life outside the school, but by life inside it, by the spirit in which this subject or that is taught, by the academic approach itself, by the status given to one subject as compared with another? Is the incapacity to believe anything enough and the suggestion that detachment alone is properly civilized related to the kind of education given, especially perhaps at the secondary and further stages?

Such questions are the more apposite to an age in which schools, without necessarily seeking to be so, are probably more powerful in their influence on boys and girls than ever before. For, as we have seen, the number staying at school to the ages of sixteen, seventeen, eighteen, is rising rapidly. The numbers taking Sixth Form courses in grammar schools are increasing by some seven per cent per year—a remarkable figure—and are likely to go on doing so. The number of those voluntarily staying on 'beyond the leaving age' in modern schools is growing fast. And one effect of the introduction of comprehensive secondary schools—whatever the merits or demerits of the principle of comprehensive schooling—will almost certainly be a still further increase in the average length of schooldays.

The greatly increased proportion of boys and girls staying on at school beyond the statutory leaving age, to sixteen and over, means that large numbers are the first generation of their families in this position. Many of them come from homes whose understanding of the function of schooling is small and whose general background of culture and knowledge is limited; and this at a time when in any case the home is apt to be more ready than in past years to contract out of what it once regarded as its own responsibilities. The attitude of many homes, well equipped with T.V. and radio sets though they may be, is that it is the school's job to educate not merely in subject-knowledge but in civilization. And this attitude is reinforced by the prevailing uncertainties concerning what it is right to believe or even take for granted.

In these circumstances the position of the secondary school is in need of re-assessment. For the task so often presented to it is not only that of giving technical education or an education to help people to pass examinations (which is itself, of course, at bottom a technical kind of education whatever the subject), but education in depth and in perception. Clearly, however, the kind of general education that is needed will not arise simply from the addition of more facts or subjects to those a boy or girl now learns. It can only come from altering the environment in which he is mentally living. And this involves the quality and kind of place a school is able to be; the 'distance' of the grown-up human beings who teach in it from the children; its discipline as well as its curriculum; and the orientation given within the teaching of subjects through which it tries to educate.

Any school is a product first and a creator second. What it can do for its pupils is largely decided by the confidence people show in it and the expectations children have of it. A great part of all the education children get is powerfully given them by the climate of opinion of their time and by life outside the school altogether. Grammar, technical, modern and comprehensive schools alike are surrounded by the hoardings and the hurry of the age.

In a hundred ways the materialist assumptions of society outside the school find their way inside. By the very fact, for instance, of gaining admission to a grammar school a boy is encouraged to be socially if soberly ambitious—and there he will learn the attitudes of other boys from middle-class homes. He will expect a life in which annual increments are the rule, and to be entitled to a pension at the end. If on the other hand he goes to a modern school, unless encouraged by parents or teachers ambitious for him, he will accept without question that he will work for wages almost as high in early life as at sixty-five.

The views of parents, teachers and adults generally about what are the desirable things in life certainly affect their children. When boys or girls leaving modern schools at fifteen or sixteen apply for jobs the first question they tend to ask is 'What about the pay?' followed by 'What are the hours?' Only much later do questions arise about the interest, type and conditions of the work to be done.

In many areas it is the tradition for mothers to earn money by working in the shops and factories, the majority part-time, but a number full-time. This means that the older girls in the family have heavy domestic duties, and this affects both their attitude towards school and the benefit they receive from the life there. Many of them arrive at the last minute in the morning because they have had to see the younger members of the family off to school. (Mother has to be in the factory at 8 a.m.). Many rush away at 4.30 p.m. in order to get the tea on the table before the parents return from work. If there is illness, or any other crisis in the family, the girls of school age stay at home and deal with the situation. Those who earn are regarded as the most important members of the family, and nothing must happen that will lessen the amount of money going into the home each week. The girls do not regard their school work and life as particularly relevant or helpful.

In all types of secondary schools, however, there can be no shadow of doubt of the power and effect of an enthusiasm on the part of the teacher, or the school tradition, over the children. It is wrong to imagine that education in school proceeds at an even pace like the weeks themselves, every day having twenty-four hours, every school day seven periods, four of, say, forty-five minutes each and three of forty. In fact education proceeds by jumps. What is being taught is by no means always what the teacher thought he was teaching; and the education of values, an essential part of which is the imparting of standards, is often the part of education which proceeds least noticeably. Standards are inhabitants of teachers' minds, not things on paper. They have to be got over as qualities, not as marks.

As everyone knows, it is possible for people to be taught over long periods in schools—whether academic or non-academic—yet to emerge only very partially educated. This may show in their spelling, their manners, the reading matter they prefer, but it shows far more in the narrowness and shallowness of their interests, and in the lack of any adequate philosophy or beliefs. A mere teaching of the doctrines of a religion, or the laws of beauty, or the rules of

geometry will not do much to help. Schools can be, and
often are, full of good teaching and yet of poor learning.
For values are to be caught not merely taught. They will
rise most fully to consciousness in the most intelligent but
they must be built into the vast majority if the life of men is
to be coherent and civilized.

'At present,' said an intelligent but critical witness to a
number of members of our committee, 'the people whom I
meet in the suburbs of the great city in which I work, even
the products of grammar school fifth forms, show some very
real deficiencies: an incapacity for objective reasoning; a
reliance on three basic principles: "What I like is beautiful;
what I think is right; what I do is good"; an incapacity for
awe or reverence before the natural world or before persons;
an inability to relax, to have leisure in the Biblical sense of
"being still," or to reflect upon their lives; and an incapacity
for creative suffering, despite much pain and anxiety. The
people who are most likely to get "lit up" are those who
have a firm hold on some "end" of man—whether Marxist,
Christian or other.'

Whatever the degree of truth in our witness's observa-
tions, it can hardly be doubted that if we are to have
citizens who can be individual and yet representative,
deeply committed though able to be detached, they must
have convictions as well as knowledge. Facts and logic are
indispensable—but they are not by themselves enough. Beliefs which are deeper than conscious reason, though not
contradicting it, must provide motive power. A religion not
true to the nature of things is doomed to fail. Perhaps the
education of mankind in religion from the primitive to the
advanced is a progress in securing recognition of what is
true—true to human perception of the good and facing
honestly the facts and laws of the natural world.

III

Many people, especially in these days, would like schools to be more powerful and successful in educating boys and girls religiously and morally, but is this part of their job? Is it not really a matter for the home? And if the home neglects its task is the school fitted anyway to tackle it? After all, school staffs are themselves largely humanist. The proportion of actively religious people among them may well be somewhat greater than in the community generally but, as far as can be seen, probably not very much greater.

Certainly the school is not a church; and certainly teachers have not the same function as parents. In the powers they should and can exercise over children, they are in fact much more representative of the community than extensions of the family; and their concern must be more with children as the representative young of the community than as individual souls to be saved. This having been said, however, there are powerful arguments that the school should take a prime part in both the religious and the moral education of children. There are several considerations to bear in mind.

First: schools cannot and ought not to trade out of the situation in which civilization finds itself. An academic detachment is not enough. Second: children equally with adults need an explanation of themselves and of the world. If schools avoid the effort of ministering to this need, they are behaving artificially. Many of the traditional sources of insight and moral guidance for our society are Christian. Third: it is accepted by almost everybody that schools should prepare children for citizenship, and necessarily embedded in this is the implication that the school should 'take sides' on many matters involving moral judgment. The time for a 'neutral' consideration whether it is desirable to be honest, to tell the truth, to think for oneself, to have a sense of responsibility, to believe in democracy, or whether it is preferable to be Mohammedan, Buddhist or Christian, may conceivably come during sixth form years or even, it may be, a little earlier. But education in citizenship for everybody up to the age of fifteen or sixteen will involve a much more convinced and 'concerned' teaching than that. Fourth: any definition of the school's function which permits it to teach only facts and skills and 'externals' confines it within limits quite unacceptable in a contemporary society. As soon, however, as a teacher becomes concerned with real life or real people he has to reckon with experiences and feelings and with the record of such experiences in literature, music or religion. The school's dealings must certainly be with 'personal knowledge' as well as objective, measurable information.

No school, even though its staff be made up of both humanists and Christians, with a very occasional atheist, can trade out of conveying values and educating the power to judge between them. In fact few teachers today, whatever their religious position, would deny that the school should play a considerable part in educating boys and girls in civilization and morality. Part of the reluctance of the humanist to go further than this in a specifically Christian direction may sometimes be due to his own inadequate perception of the importance of the 'feeling' side of education and sometimes to ignorance of what Christians believe and teach.

Many subjects will no doubt be taught without much regard to their direct moral or spiritual value. There is nothing unchristian in the idea that truth should be followed wherever it leads. 'If the choice is between believing in Christ and one's own honesty, one must choose honesty,' as Simone Weil has said. Christian integrity demands a robust honesty in scientific inquiry. But there must be no assumption that honest detachment is all that matters.

Attachment—that is, commitment—matters too, and so does readiness on the part of teachers to show that they understand this.

We may take as an example of the need for training people to be both detached and committed the education of a sense of responsibility. On the one hand, if an informed sense of responsibility is to grow, it is extremely important for the school to train minds to gather evidence, to make sure of facts. The school must impart much knowledge about things as they are, about our neighbours and the nature and history of the world in which we live. This is the context in which men make their decisions. But this sort of knowledge by itself is not enough. Even in studies at school, a mental attitude must be developed which involves personal commitment and decision, an attitude which is not content with saying 'I will look up the answer' or 'So-and-so's dictated notes will give me all I need,' but says 'I must think this out for myself.' The development of this attitude must be encouraged by suitably graded stages; but in simple ways it can hardly be started too early, plenty of support and help being given at first and the props gradually withdrawn.

The continued education of a sense of responsibility entails, however, the learning of commitments of a much wider sort. The school must provide the social framework in which children may increasingly practise the moral life and find the moral 'elbow-room' which is proper to their age. This means giving them increasing opportunities to make their own decisions; and progressively enlarging the authority they have and the weight their decisions will carry. The responsibility for managing their distribution of time—so much to be spent on this subject and so much on that—can be made increasingly theirs; they can take responsibility for running a society to give service to a group of old people or sick people; the publication of a form or school magazine can be entrusted to particular children who have shown themselves fit for the task.

The deliberate training of boys and girls to take personal and final responsibility for decisions is a very important part of moral education. There are at all stages two parts to this: exercising power to decide, and taking responsibility for what has been decided. Training in the ability to make decisions can be gradual. While in the second form boys and girls ought to decide for themselves whether, say, to start an exercise on a fresh page or not, whether to complete a piece of homework before having a game of cricket or not. By the time they reach the sixth form, boys and girls ought to be making up their minds responsibly on the merits of the books they read, on the rightness of some lines of national policy and on various possibilities in personal conduct. But in a welfare state today outside influences make it easy for the individual not to take many of the decisions he ought to take.

No doubt the school must teach many subjects at the behest of an 'outside' authority in the shape of contemporary economic and social demands. What we have to do is to prevent these from becoming the only demands we regard as important or relevant for the school to make on its pupils. The school ought to make moral and spiritual demands on them too. It is a place in which personal lives are being lived; where decisions, which are essentially decisions between values, must constantly be made.

But the Christian goes further than all this and declares that without opportunities for worship or for seeing how other Christians' lives are directed to and by God no understanding of their responsibility to God can be reached nor will the sovereignty and the grace of God in their lives be discovered. It is here that the Christian parts company with the humanist, and it is here that the Christian teacher's heaviest obligation lies. That boys and girls should become progressively aware of God as their intellectual and moral powers mature is the most difficult to fulfil of all the aims which inform Christian education.

It is easy, as we have seen, to live today in a world separated from the ultimates. Much education at home and in schools hardly deals with the imponderables, the uncertainties or the finalities of life. At least it is not difficult to avoid them if one wants—and the temper of the time, as perhaps also the choice of subjects for the curriculum, encourages such an avoidance. But religion, the Christian believes, is essentially coming up against ultimates and trying squarely to reckon with them. If this seems escapist, as it does to those who want us to concentrate on tangible things and objective propositions which can be exactly defined, it can hardly be more so than an attitude to experience which pays as little attention as possible to death, unavoidable suffering, self-sacrificing love. Before some of the most real facts of existence we are all at one in our ignorance and humanity. We are not only men, but man. But the Christian acknowledges these things and does not turn aside from them.

Christianity is not indeed primarily a learning of doctrines and then an attempt to put their consequences into the practice of living. Much more it is a learning of attitudes so that the Christian carries about with him a different set of values, a different understanding of the relative importance of things, from the non-Christian. A feeling of dependence on God, a recognition of the givenness of the world, creatureliness, humility as against self-sufficiency: these are Christian. 'We bless thee for our creation, preservation and all the blessings of this life' is a Christian prayer. To the Christian way of thinking man in himself is incomplete and insusceptible of completion. His life is given meaning not by his efforts to be materially successful —in that direction lies only an endless achievement of unsatisfaction—but by his capacity to understand and forgive, his power to trust and love, his willingness to take personal responsibility for others. These indeed, according to the Christian, are among the attributes of God himself.

CHAPTER TWO

The Christian Teacher and the School

I

THE TYPICAL school staff, as we have seen, is likely to be made up of a mixture of humanists and Christians. It is not easy to get statistics to show the relative proportion of teachers who are Christians and humanists, but in one English university where a careful enquiry was recently made in a department of post-graduate students training to be teachers, fifty-four per cent believed that they had a Christian philosophy of life, thirty-two per cent a humanist one, six per cent a materialist one, and eight per cent did not know where they stood. There is some evidence for supposing that the proportion of practising Christians on school staffs may not be over thirty per cent in these days, fifty per cent to sixty per cent being humanists or what may be called 'residual Christians.' 'In any future Christian society that I can conceive,' says T. S. Eliot, 'the educational system will be formed according to Christian presuppositions of what education—as distinct from mere instruction—is for; but the personnel will inevitably be mixed : one may even hope that the mixture may be a benefit to its intellectual vitality. The mixture will include persons of exceptional ability who may be indifferent or disbelieving; there will be room for a proportion of other persons professing other faiths than Christianity.'[1]

Certainly a Christian atmosphere is not likely to be created in a school where well-meant attempts to secure its Christian character force conscious divisions in the Com-

[1] *The Idea of a Christian Society,* p. 36.

mon Room on all the deeper issues of education. There are, as we have made clear, many issues on which the Christian and the humanist are not in conflict. It has also to be remembered that any school necessarily stands in a social context. Its head and staff do not control it alone. They are the servants of Governors or of a Local Education Authority, and must work within the limitations imposed by their regulations, except in so far as by persuasion they can obtain alterations. They have to co-operate with and as far as possible preserve the confidence of parents who may belong to one of a great variety of religious denominations but more probably to none. That being said, however, it should also be said that parents on the whole expect schools to be more Christian than they are themselves. Most parents who take a fairly salacious Sunday paper and allow their children from ten upwards to read it would be shocked if the schools encouraged the children in this practice or even approved of such a habit. Parents do genuinely want the school to set standards higher than those which they themselves live up to any longer, or indeed may ever have set for themselves.

A great many schoolmasters and schoolmistresses accept the basic truth of the Christian ethic, perhaps, not because they are church members nor because of social convenience nor for prudential reasons, but because it accords with what they believe human nature at its best to be like. The Sermon on the Mount they take to be the ideal of right human conduct though they would not accept its author as divine.

The Christian teacher, particularly if he is the head of a school, but even if he is an assistant, can do much to help his children to see the Christian presuppositions and to get an inkling of how Christianity differs from secularism. He has to do this in a society where inevitably outside influences will be making themselves much felt. There is a widespread feeling among boys and girls in the mid-twentieth century that they don't really know what they want to be or do. Aimlessness is general. The amount of pocket money given to many children in these days is considerable; with no guidance offered about how to spend it, and no long-term view, this constitutes as it were parental permission to be irresponsible to the extent of 5s. or 7s. 6d. or 10s. a week as the case may be. Many schools at the end of a term find surprisingly large numbers of unclaimed overcoats as well as caps left behind, most of them in reasonable condition. Responsibility and self-sacrifice are perhaps even more unpopular virtues than they used to be. Easy-goingness is commonly judged a highly desirable quality. And the apparently arbitrary nature of reward does little to help—double-pay on Sunday and time-and-a-half on Saturdays, with the slacker paid the same as the conscientious, and the lad of nineteen almost as much as the man of thirty-five with a growing family of four. Contained in any planning of a welfare state is the assumption that men know what kind of state is really likely to be good for their welfare; and certainly a material, irresponsible kind of welfare bulks large in the popular idea of such a state.

The consequences of such a mistaken scale of values are many. A schoolmistress who gave evidence to us wrote: 'Having recently corrected fifty-five essays of thirteen-year-olds on the events of Thursday night in Holy Week, I find all but five excuse Peter for his flight and his denials: it is painstakingly explained that had he stuck by his Master it would have been "hard on him" and his family; he might have suffered imprisonment and death and what good would that be? After all, I am told, he "did his best" to make up for it later. It is this easy going attitude that is so far removed from the outlook of one whose purpose in life is not to please himself but God. And it is an attitude that we meet daily in our work as we face the problem in class room, laboratory and playing fields, the problem of how to make young people climbers and not passengers on the roads of life.'

Religion to a great many today, both adults and children, is an external affair. They know that there is something called religion which some people really believe in, just as they know that there are churches to which some people go; they know that these people believe in a person, who—for want of a more exact word—is called God; they know that there is, or was, or is supposed to have been, someone called Christ and that there is a book called the Bible which children are expected to read in school. But the notion of personal relationship with God, or the sense of sin, or the idea of forgiveness, or the nature of prayer—these they simply do not possess. They can only with great difficulty conceive what these things mean at all. Without some imaginative understanding of their meaning, however, religion can hardly make entry. And the primary problem of the teacher who is a Christian in a secular age is how to help such an understanding to grow. Young people have a capacity for adapting themselves to different codes of socially acceptable conduct without being fundamentally affected, and some degree of adaptability is healthy. But a 'divine discontent,' an unwillingness just to 'fit in,' an awareness of falling short, is indispensable to religious development.

A large part of religious education necessarily consists of the impact made on the child by the quality of a school's corporate life, the nature of the incentives it employs, its use of rewards and punishments, the sum-total of all its personal relations, the extent to which it provides an environment in which the Christian virtues can be acquired naturally and spontaneously, and in which room is given for personal growth. Perhaps the greatest enemy to moral and religious development in the contemporary secular world is the pervading atmosphere of triviality, escapism and emptiness.

It is the general spirit of a school which in great measure decides what can easily be taught there. In some schools it is far more difficult to teach the necessity of reason or the importance of accuracy or the power of imagination or the naturalness of worship, than it is in others. Some of the more personal kinds of education at every stage cannot take place at all without affection, however indirectly that affection may be expressed. By this is meant not only an affection within the teacher for his subject but his humanity towards his children and the range and scope of that humanity. The 'spirit' of a school is the product of many influences: the relationships of head and staff, the attitude of teachers to taught, the use they make—and feel free to make—of approval and blame in various situations—their initiative and zest, the motives they habitually feel they can appeal to. For the boy or girl of fourteen to eighteen one impelling need is for human, personal affection. The highlights of school experience are friendships with contemporaries and sometimes with elders. School is a place where the effect of an adult Christian life is more obviously apparent than in most. There is certainly a great difference between the education given by a school which has little personal concern for its children as individuals and one where the individual is known and treated as a person. Among the real tests of the quality of a school is whether it helps people to know each other at more than a superficial level.

On the whole schools are more aware of the need for academic training and for giving a sound introduction to subject-study than they are of the need for education of a more personal sort. To take one example of this: children get comparatively little guidance concerning what subjects they personally should take, when there is a choice. A note may be sent home to the parents indicating the choices available, and a decision requested; or the staff themselves may make the decision. But there is quite often remarkably little discussion of the matter in personal terms or with any attempt to lay bare the factors involved in the choice to be made. There is not time for that! But this very judgment that time cannot be spared for such discussion is itself significant of what the more important parts of education are deemed to be.

Again, if schools are to be concerned to give help of a personal kind which may open up possibilities of greater religious and moral awareness, they may need more deliberately to arrange more opportunities than they have usually done for older pupils to get to know the younger ones well, to have dealings with them and to take some responsibility for them. This could be done through a house system even in a day school, and indeed much progress has been made in recent years in these things in particular schools.

But a concern for the education of the child as a person does not imply the absence of school rules and laws. A Christian certainly does not accept a perfectionist theory of human nature which looks upon goodness as a plant which will flower naturally and untended. Like St. Paul he knows, 'What I would, that do I not; but what I hate, that do I.' Children should grow up in an ordered community, which the school should seek to provide. They need protecting from the illegitimate pressures of others, and from exercising such pressures themselves. An appreciation by the individual child of his place in and of his responsibility for the well-being of his school is a first stage in the extension of his concern for others outside the limits of his family. In the school he can begin to understand what Lord Lindsay spoke of as 'the morality of our station and its duties,' and then perhaps to learn to love his neighbour and to go the second mile with him.

It would be a mistake to try to label as Christian one particular type of school government, though doubtless we should all easily identify some over-mechanised and authoritarian institution as making difficult the development of the human relationships that ought to exist in a Christian school. An over-emphasis on short term successes, whether in academic or physical pursuits, in examinations or in football matches, will produce a false set of values. This does not mean, however, that it is necessarily un-Christian to encourage boys and girls to measure themselves against each other in many fields of activity and to learn that superiority or inferiority in one of them is a matter neither for boasting nor humiliation. Natural inequalities exist among children of the same father, and can help in schools to teach St. Paul's lesson, 'God hath set the members each one of them in the body, even as it pleased Him. And if they were all one member where were the body? But now they are many members, but one body.'

The creation of a closely united school community has its own dangers. Perhaps one of the most insidious temptations of the keen schoolmaster is to over-emphasize the virtue of loyalty to the school in the attempt to create a real sense of community and to break down the self-centredness of the young. But the totalitarian school like the totalitarian state is a false god.

A school which is to give Christianity a chance will be one in which privacy can be protected, insights can happen and a wide range of experiences, not all of them just pleasurable and some of them deep, can take place. It may help these ends if both boys and girls throughout their school life are called by their Christian names. It will certainly help if recognition is quietly forthcoming for the achievement of imaginative, personal perception, whether expressed in words or action. Praise tends to be underestimated as a powerful instrument of education. The respect for imagination and spontaneity is still too low in a number of schools. Yet without spontaneity there will be little imaginative insight: 'to get used to not reacting until one is allowed is a terrible condition, the basis of evil.'

Nevertheless the school must not be weak or slack or just 'free'; and it must know how to use expectation in a deliberate way. There is certainly much less awkwardness and there are many fewer inhibitions during the adolescent period if a boy or girl knows fairly well what is expected of him, and has, or is given, a definite status in the community. Nor need there be any conflict between the possession of status and being unselfish or acting with creative purpose. It may be remarked in passing that one of the results of success in a public examination may be the gift of such status to some individuals for the first time.

Anyone who has been concerned with children soon discovers two situations in which any one of them may go to pieces. One is a feeble environment which provides no firm response to anything that he may do so that he finally becomes lost in his own waywardness with no signposts to guide him into profitable activity. The other is an environment which responds firmly but mechanically; there is no resilience, no recognition of the individual in his unique situation.

A framework of law in the school, but of law administered in a spirit of Christian love, so that the child may feel that those in authority want him to succeed as a person, cannot be dispensed with. One of the most difficult tasks for busy people in charge of schools is this creation of a sense of security and confidence, which may be shattered for a child by an unconsidered word or a hasty act. Sanctions and punishments there must be, but the wrongdoer must be studied patiently and known personally, as well as punished. One of the most serious mistakes about punishments is to assume that they are most fair when they are least personal. Children do not cease to be individuals because they do wrong, and they need more love, not less, when they prove exasperating. It may be that the actual administration of punishment should be impersonal, but, when it is over, full and personal concern for the pupil should resume sway.

One of the ways in which love will show itself in any community is in forgiveness. Although forgiveness holds a central place in Christian belief, the part that it plays in the day-to-day business of ordinary living is apt to be small. When Jesus gave the disciples the Lord's Prayer, the one clause that He reinforced with an explanatory comment was that about forgiveness, reminding them that it must always be a three-way relationship, involving myself and other people, as well as myself and God. The first experience that a child has of forgiveness is of receiving it. He upsets his relationship with his mother, and it is restored by her forgiveness. If this is to become an active, creative experience, there are two conditions to be fulfilled. In the first place, the child has to become aware that he has upset his relationship with his mother or whoever else may be involved. If he thinks he can do what he likes without affecting anyone, if there is no disciplinary framework that he knows he has broken, then he is hardly likely to realize his need of forgiveness at all, and there seem to be many children who grow up in just this condition. They are insensitive because they have never experienced a full personal relationship involving a sense of what happens if it is disturbed. In the second place the acceptance of forgiveness is an incomplete experience if it is unaccompanied by a sense of obligation to be ready to forgive. One of the most insidious cankers of evil is to turn an act of wrong-doing into a grievance. The phrase 'to nurse a grudge' is in itself a revealing expression of the temptation to tend with loving care what amounts to a perpetual excuse for behaving badly. In its developed form this is a vice more typical of adults than of children, who forgive and forget with equal ease, but the way in which children can sometimes remember years after the event even a small incident in which they seemed to be treated unjustly is a reminder of the power of the emotions which are kept in harmony by forgiveness. Within the school there must be a place for forgiveness, as distinct from willingness to forget, particularly within the dealings of teachers with taught.

Ought a Christian school to try to get rid of marks, or form orders, or end-of-term reports, on the ground that these may encourage selfish sentiments? The problem is not whether we should stop making use of competitive motives. We cannot in fact avoid making use of them. The more real problem is how we can utilise as well other motives and incentives which will put the appeal to self-interest and egotism in its place. And in this a great deal must depend upon the spirit of the school and the sheer quality of the people who teach in it. Their own hierarchy of values will inevitably shine through their actions. If at heart they believe in material success as the most important thing, their pupils will tend to regard the real business of life as the achievement of this kind of success. But if, on the other hand, parents and teachers—and others with whom they are in contact too—show that for them the true meaning of life is not to be found in such achievement, but in the winning of victories of another and deeper sort, the pupils will at least be helped to put material success and ambition into their places. What is so often needed is that the teacher, by a word in season, should show that he has recognized and appreciated at its true worth some moral achievement, some piece of unselfishness, some achievement of insight on the part of the boy or girl.

To do this necessitates a very close relationship of teacher with taught, a degree of understanding and close observation which few of us can manage for much of the time. Yet there is no possible substitute for it. Unless someone—it may not be the teacher, it may be a mother or father or friend—refuses to accept the conventional set of values and value-judgments and points to a more Christian one, the chances are enormous that a child will remain motivated chiefly by material considerations and as time goes on will lose his moral battles and become content with a lower quality of living than he might have achieved. Moments of insight will grow fewer, the everyday values of our competitive society will grow more dominant and unquestionable.

II

The choice of the actual subjects of the school curriculum, and of the content of those subjects, is much more a matter of convention than is usually thought. Possible and perhaps desirable subjects for study in school are many; but in practice they are limited to a dozen or so by three factors: there are only about thirty teaching hours in a week, the number of teachers is relatively few, and a powerful tradition exists to determine what subjects those teachers will have been trained to teach. The tradition itself is affected by subjects seen to have relevance to life or to have had such relevance in the past. English, arithmetic, science, housecraft, metalwork, social studies are in the timetable of the secondary modern school, for instance, because they have a counterpart in life and can be seen to have one.

But for many children religious knowledge or art or poetry have little apparent counterpart in the life they know: and the teaching of these subjects involves re-opening or extending ability to experience.

The bias in the secondary school today is in favour of studies which neither involve much reckoning with personal experience nor much personal ability to experience at some depth. The correction of this bias—which belongs generally to our civilization—is a matter, as far as the school is concerned, to some small extent of curriculum reform, rather more largely one of modifying the bias in approach to some of the subjects within the curriculum. At every stage there is need for children to feel the element of unchangeableness which is in life. On the personal side, any experience of love or loyalty can bring home one aspect of this unchanging permanence. But there is need also for study, within school subjects, of the unchangeable pattern of the universe—of nature (through physics, chemistry, mathematics, astronomy, geology); of human nature (much of which is expressed in literature, art and music); of history (approached as the unalterable basis on which the present is built); of God himself (recognized as fundamental reality, unaltering, to be accepted). Such implications of unchangeableness have religious connotations. The approach to many subjects of the curriculum can help or hinder the growth of a spiritual sense. Certainly the secular assumptions quietly taken for granted in our teaching of science or literature or social studies often matter very much indeed.

The justification for including a subject in the curriculum may well not be primarily the objective knowledge it gives the learner but its ability to extend or modify presuppositions. Today there is a decided tendency to regard all knowledge as really technical in character. Even history, music, literature and religious knowledge are often approached as if they were studies of this sort. But however many facts have to be mastered in studying a subject it is not they which are educative in themselves. It is no doubt easier to teach science in 1960 than religious knowledge because the climate of opinion outside as well as inside schools and universities is so favourable. But the scope of education must be large enough to include the nourishment of imagination, trust and worship if it is to activate us at sufficient depth. Much education must necessarily be largely an education in recognition—in recognition of the significance of this or that piece of experience we have already encountered.

The secularism of our age is in part due to our lack of perception of the range and profundity of our own natures. We concentrate attention on the conditions in which we live rather than acknowledge the validity of our sympathies and see the significance of our own good impulses. Yet, as Joyce Cary says, a man (and the same is true of a child) 'is more directly aware of unselfish affection, of the movement of his own sympathies, than of the constitution of the atom. For anyone to cut himself off from any point of contact with the actual world, from any experience of its nature, religious, aesthetic or scientific is to stultify his mind and starve his imagination.' Darwin concentrated on investigating the conditions of evolution, and did not perceive that it could only be *understood* from within as well as from without, moral and imaginative insight being a step in man's evolution itself. He did not see the significance of the truth that unselfish goodness—including an outstandingly unselfish goodness in himself—exists in human nature and therefore in universal nature : a fact as valid as any observation of science and more immediate. Experience remains as important as experiment.

Facts, important and interesting though they are, are

sometimes even more significant as symbols. Take gesture as a very simple instance of this. The gesture itself is a fact to be observed—the bend of an arm, the light in an eye, the contortion of a face—but the significant thing is the meaning it conveys. Appearance and behaviour, whether in animals or human beings, are not only facts but indications of temper, mood and idea. Many facts are important both in themselves and for what they symbolise. Dress, language, lilt, silence, ritual are none of them simply facts-to-be-observed in detachment. They all convey intention, meaning, spirit, and if we are to perceive this we must be involved first even if we are detached second.

The suggestion is that again and again within the teaching of any subject is concealed the teaching of important presuppositions—some of which will help and some of which may hinder or prevent the growth of any vital or religious understanding. Most subjects are most successful in educating presuppositions when learning them is a group experience. 'We learn history from historians, as we learn science from scientists, as we learn goodness from good people,' says Lord Lindsay. Standards are learned from people who possess and incorporate them. Standards in learning history or science 'imply in all cases a society inspired by the same spirit, attaining a standard which is both traditional and creative. The maintenance of standards in scientific or historical work is a delicate business. It depends upon the continued behaviour of a certain kind of society, a society of scientists or a society of historians, and the more perfectly this kind of society is maintained the more science and history are found to apprehend, though imperfectly, the reality towards which their investigations are directed.'[1] Standards of goodness are learned in the same way.

[1] *Selected Addresses*, pp. 151-52.

A school which is content only to fit in with convention and to teach facts and skills, deductions and foreseeable consequences is not giving its boys and girls the orientation they need if they are to be Christians in a period like ours. A contemporary school is not likely to be a community of Christians in Eliot's sense, but in its general spirit and its teaching of most subjects it can do much to foster a humility of mind and spirit, to encourage a recognition of the givenness of things and to help people to take for granted the value of imaginative understanding. And these perceptions are consistent with a Christian approach. To a consideration of the teaching of some individual subjects we must now turn.

CHAPTER THREE

The Approach to Mathematics and Science

No MATTER what subject a master or mistress teaches, he cannot in fact teach that subject only. If he could, school-mastering would certainly be a less hazardous trade than it is. Unavoidably a teacher of any subject will be transmitting attitudes too; with no consciousness that he is doing so, he may be teaching attitudes which make easy or difficult an understanding that life is more than an interplay of inevitable and material forces.

Mathematics and science now have an assured place in the curriculum of all secondary schools and that place is growing larger. During the last fifty years, and particularly since the end of the first world war, their importance in the schools has increased, so that now it is common to find that more than one-third of the timetable in the secondary modern school and the middle forms of grammar schools is devoted to mathematics and science, and on the science sides of the Sixth Forms the proportion is very much greater. This development is a natural, but not a consciously planned, outcome of the increasing impact of science and the scientific and rationalistic (or sometimes pseudo-rationalistic) modes of thought that are such an important feature of the recent history of western civilization. The teaching and learning of the sciences and of mathematics can easily make all considerations of value seem irrelevant. The science teacher can so easily convey—without meaning to do so—the idea that emotional and aesthetic judgments are unimportant, and ethical and moral considerations unreal, that

Christians cannot merely accept without question and proper discussion the place of science in education. The battle for the Christian point of view may largely be fought in the science classroom.

What are the main justifications for the inclusion of mathematics and science in the curriculum? In the past, the inclusion and retention of certain subjects in the time-table have sometimes been justified on the grounds of the mental training they supposedly provided. The conclusions of experimental psychologists have overthrown many of the arguments of this nature that formerly carried weight : automatic transfer would not now be acceptable as the justification for including, to take one instance, formal geometry in the curriculum. But without doubt the discipline of study of mathematics provides one of the testing grounds for the human intellect. To experience something of the thrill of mathematical or scientific discovery, to 'rethink the thoughts of the great' in these as in many other fields of human endeavour can come within the scope of most children. This attitude of mind on the part of the educator provides some part of the justification, for example, of our experimental approach in the teaching of science and of problem work in mathematics.

Again, science and mathematics, particularly in our own time, are undoubtedly admirable subjects for bringing home to the student the sheer importance of accuracy. Here much will depend upon the precision and controlled enthusiasm of the teacher himself. Accuracy, whether in the exact expression of meaning through words or in the conduct of an experiment, is not the outcome of 'teaching' merely, but is partly the result of absorbing what is 'in the air' of the school or classroom where the teaching is going on.

But the main justification for an important place for science and mathematics in the curriculum is that the world in which we live is of such complexity that no child can really take his place in it without a good deal of scientific and mathematical knowledge. Science is here to stay: if we are to remain contemporary and really belong to the twentieth century, we must be interested in it. The penalty for not being interested is to cut ourselves off from our civilization as it is developing, and therefore from humanity too. We are still near the beginning of its influence both on our daily lives and, more subtly, on our way of looking at things. This is a much more important reason for studying science than the argument that only so can the country be kept prosperous—though the reasons are not as separate as might at first appear. To prepare children to take their place in this highly complex technological world is not of course a matter only of acquiring elementary mathematical and scientific skills. Indeed, a detailed consideration of this aspect of the problem would probably show that for the great majority of citizens a very small deposit of mathematical and scientific knowledge would be called for. The case of the future specialist, the engineer, the industrial scientist, or applied mathematician, is different. To consider it would open up the whole question of vocational and specialized training. But if the actual amount of knowledge and skill of a scientific or mathematical kind that must be acquired by everybody is small, the needs of the community, or at any rate of a democratic community, include considerable understanding and appreciation by everyone of the implications of science in modern life. It is here that our schools too frequently fail in their tasks. It is certainly possible for science teachers, and the boys and girls they teach, to go on living essentially in pre-scientific forms of thought and make use of the results of science 'as formerly primitive people made use of European top hats, Albert chains and glass beads.' Working under the shadow of the examination syllabus, with an almost inevitable emphasis upon those things that are more easily tested by written papers, facts rather than principles become the dominant features of the teaching, a tendency aggravated by the rapidly increasing bulk of the work regarded as coming within the elementary field. A knowledge of the material universe will lead on to the control of it, to a lesser or greater degree, and this control, unless it is guided by forces of a moral or ethical kind, can be used as readily for the promotion of evil as of good. The Christian teacher and the Christian school, while conceding the rights of the community in its demands upon the scientific part of the curriculum, cannot stand aside from the responsibility to criticize the standards of the community; neither can they ignore the direction in which the community is moving.

The content of the syllabuses in mathematics and science is bound, then, to be dictated very largely by the needs of the contemporary and probable future form of organized society. When the extent and scope of the subjects are being determined a teacher's comment will hardly be affected by the fact that he is a Christian—though his approach to the teaching of them will be. The good teacher, whether Christian or humanist or pagan, will of course be concerned with more than the acquisition of skills; he will be anxious to make clear the underlying principles of his subject, and to exhibit its elegancies. He will be aware, for example, of the importance of pattern and of getting the *feel* of pattern in learning mathematics, that the idea of a variable is an idea which is intriguing to the imagination. (Mathematics indeed involves the constant invention of artificial worlds because the real world is too complex.) He will also demand from his pupils those moral qualities necessary for good academic work. Though there is scarcely a 'Christian' mathematics or a 'Christian' science, the Christian teacher will often find himself placing a different emphasis upon, and—almost without knowing that he does so—giving a different weighting to some parts of the subject than will an agnostic. In mathematics, particularly where the question of the nature of proof arises, he will never lose sight of the fact that proof may be of different kinds according to the nature of the subject matter. And he will show his pupils that he realizes this. Proof of a kind that is appropriate in the field of mathematics cannot be expected in, for example, the critical study of Biblical text. And the kind of proof that the mystic finds convincing as a result of his deep spiritual experiences, which is so private in nature, is in no way akin to the more public form of proof that is capable of being laid before all comers. The real danger is that the power of deductive reasoning, particularly when it is dealing with very elementary mathematical ideas, may so take hold of a boy or girl that the results of any intellectual processes that are of a different kind will be rejected as entirely inadequate.

It is extraordinarily comforting when one feels ill and suspects that one may have a temperature to make a test with a clinical thermometer and find that one hasn't. The evidence is—within its limits—objective, final. Such an indisputable verdict is of the kind we would all much like to be able to have about many matters in life. But thermometers and science itself are essentially concerned with the measurable, not with convictions, evaluations, aesthetic judgments, which belong to the inward life of the individual. For science as such there are no mysteries, however many there may be for the scientist as a man: it either deals with mysteries by making them into problems, or leaves them outside its orbit. Science well taught must make learners aware that it has such limitations of function and range. The claim that science accepts no presuppositions and is therefore superior to a Christianity which does is wholly false. That nature is knowable and that natural law works uniformly are themselves suppositions which scientific method by itself cannot prove. Yet if they are not true, the scientists' whole work must be subject to much discount. Science assumes the rationality of the universe and selects data which rationality can deal with.

An important difference between the reasoning of mathematics and science should be recognized. When a boy finds, by measurement, that the sum of the angles of a triangle is $179\frac{1}{4}°$ (if such accuracy were possible), we say 'So much the worse for your experiment.' When he finds a comparable error in Boyle's Law we say 'So much the worse for Boyle's Law.' The *idea* in mathematics is the truth (for the boy can know nothing of non-Euclidean geometrics); in mathematics one starts with axioms and postulates. But in science the *facts,* not the hypotheses, are sacred. One begins with as many of the facts as can be gathered and uses inductive reasoning to arrive at generalizations or principles. Whether in mathematics the idea of an Absolute is pre-figured is a moot point; certainly science knows an objective world to which we need to conform.

In all teaching it is worth while on occasion to analyse the methods actually in use. An instance may help: when a boy is first learning about movements—say he is solving the problem of reactions when a car is on a bridge—two features of the solution should be brought out.

1. Forces are treated as having 'lines of action' (and the car becomes a point); a simplification of the 'it is as if' sort, for they are pressures spread over an area.

2. The make and colour of the car, even whether it will go, are irrelevant for the purpose.

Many later difficulties will be avoided if the boy appreciates the reasons for simplification and selection, and that what is omitted may for other purposes be the important factors in the situation.

In the physical sciences there are more obvious implications for the Christian. The root of the matter lies in the essential attitudes to be adopted towards the material universe. A question that the Christian teacher of science must frequently ask himself and sometimes ask his pupils is: what is the nature of the physical world? Is matter 'primary stuff,' beyond which there is no reality? or is the world of space and time only one part of the creation, and a less important part at that? The so-called 'laws of nature' must from time to time be examined for what they are—in most cases the filtered deposit from experience and experiment on which can be built knowledge and control of future events. Such forecasts and controls are based upon probability, probability of a very high order indeed, but probability and not certainty. It is a tempting thought to the youngster surrounded by the dazzling glare of scientific discoveries and conquests to believe that, just as the astronomer can usually foretell to the fraction of a second the positions and movements of the planets, enough scientific knowledge and patience would enable us to solve similar problems in the realm of human conduct. But the findings of the physical sciences, or for that matter of psychology and sociology, do not rule out the possibility of free will for man in some measure at least. The Christian teacher himself will probably have entertained at one time or another—he may still do so on occasion—all the doubts and uncertainties that will inevitably assail his pupils in the issue between determinism and free-will. The right word spoken, either to a class or to an individual pupil, may be of immense importance in the developing spiritual growth of a child meeting these intellectual difficulties for the first time.

Any humane approach to the teaching of science must

cultivate a sense of the continuity of nature on a non-materialistic basis. A persistent creative trend such as the development of the world manifests cannot be accounted for in terms of mere accident.

In the biological sciences, most obviously of all, fundamental problems are presented which cannot be escaped from by the Christian teacher—and should not be avoided by the non-Christian either. Whereas the physicist and chemist may appear to be considering the nature of the 'primary stuff' of the universe, the biologist clearly comes much closer to dealing with the problem of the relationship of man to the remainder of the animal world. The most obvious problems that arise from the evolutionary theory will call for bold yet sympathetic handling. In focusing attention on the *conditions* of evolution we must never forget its actuality.[1] And no amount of study of the 'facts' of an animal's or a plant's structure can be any substitute for an understanding of what it feels like to live and grow and evolve. It is important in the school to give opportunities to boys and girls to enter into the existence of other living things, to cultivate an imaginative understanding of what 'facts' actually mean. The keeping of pets can have great educational value. But children need to get to know animals more than either as pets or as potential subjects for dissection.

Strong though man's ties with the lower animals are, however, the Christian cannot accept the thesis that man is merely an animal. The essential differences between man and the animals, particularly in so far as these relate to his power to discriminate between good and evil and his all too frequent choice of an evil course of action, should find their place in the biology class as well as in the more formal parts of the Divinity syllabus.

[1] Cf. M. Polanyi: *Personal Knowledge* (London, 1958), pp. 347-405.

Again, the question whether man's appearance on the earth was merely the result of a series of fortuitous accidents, or whether it was part of a larger pattern, may well arise in biology. The Christian gives a clear answer here. In giving such an answer he places in its proper perspective many other problems relating to man's attitude towards, and responsibility for the right use of, the world in which he lives, including non-living things as well as the living creatures.

A hundred years ago a great battle was being fought between Science and Religion. There is no doubt that much intolerance and lack of understanding of the fundamental problems at issue were shown by the contestants on both sides. That battle is over (or its first round is). Theologians and scientists of the twentieth century can for the most part appreciate the fact that their respective methods of study and the kinds of questions each asks and answers are at once irreconcilable and yet entirely compatible. They may sometimes indeed be complementary. The inevitable time-lag between the points of view of the experts and the knowledge possessed by the man in the street means that some of the old battlefields of the nineteenth century may have to be fought over again in the minds of the intelligent, but only partly-informed, child. The problems, for example, which arise out of a study of the early chapters of Genesis are hardly likely to arouse any serious difficulties, except in the minds of that very small proportion of children brought up in the homes and denominations where extreme literalism is adopted in the study of the Bible. Where there is honest doubt or difficulty of this kind, sensible co-operation between the teachers of science and of Divinity can usually help the child to a resolution of his intellectual dilemma. Doubt, if accompanied by humility, is often a creative condition of mind. Donne's words spring to remembrance:

Doubt wisely; in strange way
To stand inquiring right is not to stray;
To sleep, or run wrong, is. On a huge hill
Cragged and steep, Truth stands, and he that will
Reach her, about must and about must go,
And what th' hill's suddenness resists, win so.

More important than any active antagonism between science and religion are the emotional attitudes engendered by concentration on the applications of science—its technologies and its material benefits. Such attitudes are subtly materialistic and often militate against a spiritual view of life by implying that it is unnecessary. It is here that a recognition of the selective character of the data of science is important.

The problem today is different from that of the nineteenth century, yet in essence it has been with man ever since he became a moral being. The teacher of science, and to a smaller degree of mathematics also, will seek to encourage his pupils, by many opportunities that occur in the classroom and laboratory, to see himself in a spirit of humility as a child of God, recognising that his Father in Heaven is the Creator of all things. Reverence for inanimate things, reverence for the animal kingdom, reverence for other men, derive from, and are expressions of, that sense of God's love for each one of us which demands in return man's dedication of himself to God's purposes that is the ultimate aim of all Christian education.

There is no gainsaying that the utilisation of scientific knowledge for material ends, together with the need for securing good examination results, are among the main dangers to the science teacher. He becomes fearful of irrelevance and of wasting time if he spends precious minutes in dealing with the origins or history of science, its impact upon civilization, its relationship with religion, or the limitations of the relevance of the methods it uses.

References to the history of science are important in teaching not so much for themselves as for their help to the pupil in seeing what science is about. And this is important even if our aim is to produce more people who are really scientists or technologists instead of more and more who 'know' science or 'know' technology. Experiments which go on in the mind are more significant educationally than experiments which go on in the laboratory—though not a substitute for them. To go back in teaching a particular topic in mathematics or in science to the period when the theorem or law was first discovered is often brightly illuminating. This may help children to capture something of the spirit in which the discovery was made and to give them a sense that at a particular time in history such developments 'had to come,' with events steadily building up to the moment of discovery. It will certainly help them to understand that the scientist's thinking is not purely logical. He is man as well as measurer. He works with presuppositions, has hunches, must make decisions between almost equally tempting lines of evidence, must have faith and use intuition.

'Think for a moment,' says Professor C. A. Coulson, 'of some of the attitudes of mind with which any scientist comes to his search: there is honesty, and integrity, and hope: there is enthusiasm, for no one ever yet began an experiment without an element of passion: there is an identification of himself with the experiment, a partisan character about his secret hope for its conclusion which not even an adverse result can wholly extinguish: there is a humility before a created order of things which are to be received and studied: there is a singleness of mind about the search which reveals what the scientist himself may often hesitate to confess, that he does what he does because it seems exciting and it somehow fulfils a deep part of his very being: there is co-operation with his fellows, both in the same laboratory, and across the seven seas: there is patience, akin to that which kept Mme. Curie at her four years' self-imposed task of purifying eight tons of pitch-blende to extract a single gramme of radium: above all there is judgment—judgment as to what constitutes worth-while research: judgment as to what is fit and suitable for publication. No wonder that a modern scientist—and no Christian either—has to say that "science cannot exist without judgments of value".'

Intuitive thinking is indispensable to science. In a sense the scientist is like the actor in using his imaginative understanding, though he or the spectator of his acting may build the logical framework afterwards. The 'public facts' of science are not *entirely* public, though the scientist must act for most of the time as if they were. We shall certainly not have succeeded in our science teaching if we induce a frame of mind in our pupils which rules out in their minds the validity of moments of 'revelation' in scientific research or discovery. To regard science teaching as the covering of a syllabus—getting always on and on—may well prevent the coming into being of a state of mental relaxation in which fundamentals can be grasped. And the fundamentals are not only or purely intellectual. Rutherford, it is said, had almost an affection for beta particles. There is a vast difference between saying: 'We'll teach science because it is one of the best ways of keeping a boy mentally alive and making him educated'; and 'We'll teach science because this is in the long run the means to make our country prosperous.'

The Christian teacher of science will not teach facts or theories in any essentially different way from the humanist or non-Christian but he will make clear to his pupils, in ways such as have been suggested, that he is aware of the limitations of the scientific approach as well as its indispensable value. Certainly, as Dr. J. Bronowski has pointed out, the language of science must be made part of the cultural education of all young people. But we shall depend on the width and depth of the science teacher's own philosophy of life to save his teaching from closing the minds of his pupils to both the compatibility and the necessity of beliefs other than scientific.

The more widely and profoundly concerned about life a science teacher is, the less dangerous is it for him to teach his particular subject—provided that he is willing to reveal himself from time to time as a human being, showing that he is concerned about general moral questions, about metaphysics, about matters of religious belief, in other words about problems which he knows to be really human problems. He must not be afraid to give glimpses of himself as a complete adult man as well as a scientist. The point is made by F. B. Welbourn when he says: 'The man who taught me physics also took me sailing and invited me to his house to hear records on a gramophone. His sailing and his music were used to illustrate his lectures in physics; his physics enriched his appreciation of his leisure activities. There was, one felt, a similar integration between all these activities and his enthusiasm as a husband and father, a churchman, a social worker and a politician. He was, in fact, a whole man. But, despite the deep enthusiasm for a total scientific approach to life which characterises, for instance, the members of the Association of Scientific Workers, it is precisely that sense of wholeness which is largely missing from so many students of science. They listen to good music, they read modern poetry, they may even follow an explicitly religious group—frequently of a wholly irrational character.

But these activities are patently an escape from the emotionally unsatisfying drudgery of professional work.'[1]

It is certainly impossible to teach science or mathematics humanely if those teaching it are not humane. It may well be that the philosophy and history of science will not appeal to the science teacher; that is as it may be. What matters more is that some of the problems of humanity itself should appeal to him and that his approach to teaching should not cause him to conceal himself as a man by pretending to be nothing but a teacher—or a scientist.

Science and Humanity, p. 112.

CHAPTER FOUR

Literature and the Arts

LITERATURE is concerned not merely with people but with people at their most personal. That is one reason why reading it can make us face the facts about human nature and the human spirit instead of remaining content to understand it at a much more superficial level. It is not primarily because so much of English literature is informed by Christian values—though that is undoubtedly true—nor because some of it is overtly religious that we want boys and girls to read it, but because they cannot be simply detached or escapist when they really read a good book. Literature and art too are concrete, not abstract: even when they deal with general problems they deal with them in particular, individual instances. Ideas of integrity, of guilt, sin, atonement, forgiveness may be grasped and accepted from Dickens or Shakespeare or Conrad or Hardy without defences being raised, when the same ideas direct from the teacher might appear to have an element of preaching or special pleading, which would be suspect. Literature really steeps the mind in 'la condition humaine.' It can bring one face to face with realities that are basic, with love, death and destiny, war and peace; the boy or girl who has had a glimpse of some of the implications in, say, Shakespearian tragedy may possibly approach more sympathetically the mystery of the crucifixion and resurrection.

Here of course may be a source for an interest in philosophy, in the sense of an inquiry into what life is about. We shall not, however, expect the reading of literature to make people 'better' so much as 'bigger'. The important thing to have in mind when dealing with literature or any other forms of art is that they convey experience as experience, bringing with them the tang and taste of life, disciplining the attentive spirit by their facing of the ways in which men live and things happen. By this means the spirit is stretched and grows. Life itself often teaches us things before we are quite ready for them and we call this very process the discipline of life. Works of art can have the same kind of disciplinary effect.

As A. I. Richards says, 'facts properly documented are comforting things in an age which does not know what it is doing or in what to put its faith . . . (But) facts are no true comforts until we know how to take them; and that is just our problem.'[1] We need not only to learn facts but what the facts mean, to learn, that is, how to interpret them in relation to one another. While the first object of teaching literature and the arts in the school may be to enlarge the range and number of the experiences coming in to our lives, inseparable from this process is the ordering of such experiences as they flow. Every play or painting or piece of music orders its material as it records it; if it is good, it has shape and is an indication of how one civilised, intelligent human being has taken events in his life and found coherence and meaning in them.

Progress in reading is a progress in interpreting and understanding and evaluating: from

> 'The cat sat on the mat'

through

> 'With greedy eye he look'd on all he saw,
> He knew not justice, and he laughed at law.'

to

> 'The moving moon went up the sky
> And nowhere did abide.'

[1] *Speculative Instruments*, p. 101.

From

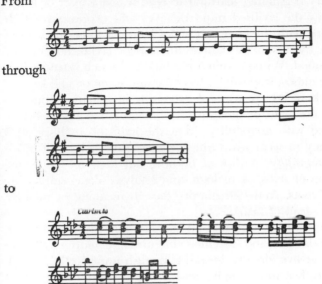

through

to

An indispensable preliminary to the study of literature, whether in English or a foreign language, is learning to read. And many children entering the secondary school can barely do that: vast numbers indeed, especially of boys, leave school just at the point when they can begin to read with profit. There is a sense in which to teach reading is a fundamental Christian duty because so much Christian teaching has been overtly expressed in words. Though mass Christian education in many ages was done without the use of the written word—through stained-glass windows, mystery plays and the drama of church services—there will be no return to those days. The way of consciousness is the way of literacy: in modern conditions people who cannot read easily are doomed to feel a permanent inferiority. From the very beginning, learning to read a text is part of learning how the civilised mind behaves and expresses itself. It is in line with the later process of learning to be the kind of person by whom the Christian basis of civilization can be understood. Without much reading and much listening that will be almost impossible. Reading and listening and looking at works of art are ways of exercising imagination and feeling. 'I now saw, or thought I saw, what I had always before received with incredulity—that the habit of analysis has a tendency to wear away the feelings,' says J. S. Mill in his *Autobiography*. A diet of nothing but facts or simply the learning of skills, or of logic and analysis alone, starves life at the roots. And Christianity has no meaning or message for the dead of heart.

It is tempting to think that the discipline given by English studies is first and foremost linguistic. Children come to school at five already speaking English imperfectly, though often rather intriguingly, and using it as the medium of their communication with one another; and since, at fifteen even, mastery of it is still distressingly limited, it is easy to understand why it should be urged that the first and overwhelmingly the most important part of an English master's job is to ensure that his pupils use English more correctly, learn with gradually increasing subtlety and delicacy what is 'the done thing,' and improve their accuracy and exactitude in reading and listening and writing. All these technical matters *are* extremely important. Listening and writing and reading are skills which have to be learnt with a hard yet delighted application if they are to be mastered in high degree.

But none of these is the most distinctive discipline brought by English into education in schools. Important, yes; essential, yes. But these skills are so various yet fundamental that they are the responsibility of others on the staff almost as much as of the teacher of English. The ability consciously to acquire and pass on information and objective facts through words becomes more and more necessary to living life in a modern age. The use of the mother tongue as a medium for the exact description of a process must certainly be a concern of the teacher of science or housecraft or woodwork; the art of summarising the concern of the teacher of history or geography; learning about grammatical function the province of those who teach French, and so on. Every teacher is a teacher of English so far as teaching to listen, to speak, to read, to write are concerned.

The distinctive contribution of English is of a different kind. What we are after through the study of literature is bringing to consciousness in our pupils what is involved in being human. One of the prime purposes is to enlarge insight into human motive; to increase the range and profundity of understanding of human character; gradually to improve ability to judge the depth and scope of the experiences a boy or girl gets from reading and listening to literature. The good reader may not approve of Hamlet's murder of his stepfather but he must have sympathy with Hamlet even as the murder is being done; he may not himself be old as he reads *King Lear* but he must know what it feels like to be old. Only a person who has felt for himself widely and deeply in this way can have the materials to make good moral judgments in many situations should he need (and he often will need) to do so. Lacking the experience which reading literature or looking at pictures brings he will judge human conduct on inadequate evidence. Colour prejudice, lack of understanding of foreigners, or of people who are old, or poor, or rich, is the direct outcome of inexperienced, unexercised imagination. The alternative to not being experienced at heart is not being experienced at all. If we do not accept life there is nothing to accept in its place. What idea of essential *man* does a boy or girl get from the material provided by newspapers, comics, advertisements, science fiction and T.V.? And without a perception of what man is really like, religious perception will be prevented or starved.

The main direction of English teaching should be from experiencing, through comprehension, to evaluation. But the primary need is that of experiencing. The fundamental sin of the teacher of literature is that he should get in the way and prevent that from happening when a pupil reads a book. For most people, even in adolescence, life quickly and easily becomes just a series of events. The capacity for experiencing becomes overlaid and part of the whole capacity to learn is deadened. It is because of this that young people become so bored. Boredom descends readily in these days, and entertainment—often of a rather exaggerated or sub-human kind—has to be provided (usually by other people) to get rid of it.

In the mid-twentieth century it is far more necessary to read literature in order to remain in touch with life and other people than it was in a more primitive society. For the very artificiality and isolation in which civilised men live separate them from experiences which once they would have encountered by proximity. Reading literature is certainly no substitute whatever for living, but it is a means by which living can be made more real, and the scope of man's powers and the tragedy of his situation more fully apparent. The literature studied in schools must not of course be limited to Christian writers—though much of what is written by authors living in a society so much influenced by Christianity as ours will need some understanding of Christianity for its apprehension. Nor must the literature read be judged too narrowly by moral criteria. Many of the objections to the arts made by 'moralists' are expressions of fear by those who are afraid to be really disinterested because of what might happen to their moral code if they were. God could descend into Hell unscathed, and poetry or music or sculpture can for a while put us into so godlike a condition that we can wander almost anywhere serene. It is only when a moralist has little imagination that he objects to art and to poetry, and, not being able to acclimatise himself to the mountain air, assumes that everyone suffers from the same mountain sickness as himself. He has, in fact, too primitive a conception of life and morals—a conception that has no place for values other than moral values. He would sacrifice beauty, because the goodness of beauty is not moral goodness.

The arts are important subjects in the curriculum not simply because their territory is wide but because it is three-dimensional, having depth as well as length and width. For they are 'educators of the sentiments' and can feed parts of the mind more fundamental and indispensable even than the ability to reason. Consider literature in particular. Sometimes both prose and verse simply convey facts with economy and memorableness; and style, as Dorothy Emmet has brilliantly remarked, is always the feather on the arrow, not the feather in one's cap. But at other times words and sentences are not only a means of communication at a conscious level: they are also swift, unerring media through which unconscious, or all but unconscious, implication and suggestion and passion and power can be transferred from one human being to another.

Not that words and sentences alone have this ability. Some myths and stories come, as it were, out of the ancient mind of the race, revealing to us parts of our own humanity which we did not know, expressing to us portions of the unconscious which cannot find expression except in such a form.

> 'Footfalls echo in the memory
> Down the passage which we did not take
> Towards the door we never opened
> Into the rose-garden.'

Much of literature, like much of life, brings us to the discovery that we were here, so to speak, before we actually got here. 'We always understand more than we actually know.' In other words, we come upon and recognize truth as we read; the reading of great literature can bring with it humility and humanity, and create them in us.

'The true aim of literary studies,' said C. S. Lewis on one occasion, 'is to lift the student out of his provincialism by making him the spectator, if not of all, yet of much, time and existence. The schoolboy is taken by it out of the narrowness of his own age and class into a more public world. History alone will not do, for it studies the past mainly in secondary authorities. It is possible to do history for years without knowing at the end what it felt like to be an Anglo-Saxon thane, a cavalier, an eighteenth-century country gentleman. The gold behind the paper currency is to be found, almost exclusively, in literature.' Of course, in actual fact, many teachers of history use literature just for this purpose.

The Christian teacher of English is first and foremost trying to develop an *understanding* of humanity—whether he be teaching Wordsworth or Dylan Thomas, Dickens or Hardy, Shakespeare or Pepys or Burke. The types of comprehension he is anxious to develop are a good deal wider than logical comprehension alone. Involved in the appreciation of great literature is much human sympathy and a delicate exercise of imaginative perception. Really to read even Jane Austen demands a thousand nuances of apprehension; to understand Shakespeare a great openness to human experience. And there is for many people a direct carry-over from such appreciative reading to life itself. There is a sense in which literature indeed is more real than life. The purpose of education, Lord Percy of Newcastle once remarked, is to help people to judge rightly without enough evidence to do so. For life only rarely presents us with a case where a calm, detached, slow judgment is possible. Nearly always the situation is emotionally coloured. We believe that the emotional character of the pupil's response to literature in itself gives us an opportunity for helping him to develop the ability to think well under the sort of circumstances life so often presents. What he needs is not only knowledge *about* life and things and people but knowledge *of* them. He needs to be able to think and to feel at the same time.

A close, almost a loving, examination of individual words and phrases and sentences is indispensable to exactitude and faithfulness in getting to many a good author's meaning. And such an examination is impossible without a more wide-ranging understanding of the whole. It simply cannot be done if no love is there, if the thing has become a task, a purely intellectual analysis.

> 'It is the cause, it is the cause, my soul—
> Let me not name it to you, you chaste stars!
> It is the cause.'

Why should Othello call it the cause and not define it more closely?

> 'Yet I'll not shed her blood
> Nor scar that whiter skin of hers than snow
> And smooth as monumental alabaster.'

The force of *scar, alabaster;* and above all, *monumental*— does the child perceive something of it? A loving examination of words: that is one of the things we want to secure. Certainly in many contexts statements that are objectively true can be false to the intensity of what we want to say.

The good teacher of English and the arts must inevitably today become in the course of his work the transmitter of an unfamiliar, since unfashionable, set of values, just because literature is concerned so deeply with life: with motives, presuppositions, ideals, characters. His very choice of books for study implies a series of judgments. Why Shakespeare and not J. B. Priestley? Why Milton rather than Pope? Why Emily Brontë and not Ethel M. Dell? The commentary upon literature which matters most is not really very much concerned with things literary, but concerned very much indeed with things vital. The acquirement of critical standards is dependent upon the existence in the mind of a hierarchy of values which has been slowly created not merely out of much reading of good books, but out of much savouring and understanding of life itself and willingness to submit to what life can teach. There is no contradiction between the experiences which life brings and those given by books; the two react upon one another and the richness of each is apt to be determined by the richness of its fellow.

The function of poetry, painting, music and sculpture is not to be beautiful, though beauty may be a symptom of their attainment of one sort of perfection. Poetry and drama —to say nothing of the other arts—give experiences which may not even be pleasurable. To describe the seeing of Macbeth as necessarily a pleasant experience seems an unwarrantable misapplication of the word. In reading about Lady Macbeth we are not made more like her but more like ourselves. And the same is true, in an appropriately less degree, of much minor poetry and drama; we come back into the world of everyday, feeling that life is a more vivid and vital business than we knew. We are not necessarily more moral for having read the poem or seen the play, but we are more awake and aware.

It is this ability of art of all kinds to quicken the spirit to a high degree of awareness that no moralist is able to gainsay. In a world of daily life a thousand practical considerations and dangers make it impossible for such valuable states to come often. We cannot be detached in spirit frequently because necessities of the body, which are spiritually almost irrelevant, continually demand our attention. Poetry and the arts can temporarily deprive us of the need for responsibility for the management of our lives, our investments and our ambitions. We are able by the help of the arts to see into the life of things, just because our effort now is no longer to do anything, but only to allow ourselves to see. In a state of appreciation we are sincere and disinterested to a degree otherwise hardly possible. We accept the poet's or the artist's vision not for the sake of anything but just in and for itself.

The greater the work of art the greater the degree to which our minds are organized under its influence. We are ourselves fulfilled, instead of merely fulfilling ourselves by labour and action. A great poem does not so much satisfy reason as bring it to birth within us. Imagination, says Wordsworth,

> '. . . is but a name for absolute power,
> And clearest insight, amplitude of mind,
> And Reason in her most exalted mood.'

But, as he says elsewhere, it is necessary to imagine 'in a wise passiveness.' Unless we exclude moral considerations from our approach to a piece of music or a work of art or a poem it will be impossible to come to it thus wisely. If we are always striving to find some moral in what a great writer wrote, we shall sacrifice the spirit to the letter. And by lacking imagination we shall fail to get into touch with the real meaning of what is around us.

As was hinted earlier, the choice of texts for reading and study in the English period—as of paintings in the art period or compositions in the music period—must not be limited to the explicitly Christian. One test for such choice is the sheer vitality of a book or work of art; another is its suitability for study by adolescents.

The vitality of a piece of literature is shown by its stamina. Its life lies locked in the words. And it persists, never becoming exhausted, continually able to offer something, not necessarily the same thing, since the reading of a text must be an active process to which the reader contributes an active, creative part. Vitality shows itself in the power to engage the attention at many levels. It can minister to the innocent, to the experienced and to the disillusioned. And it manifests itself in contemporaneity, in being able to touch and enlighten the human situation today, that human situation which lies below the accidents of fashion and the externals of period. It is not those texts which are most explicitly valuable to historians, not even those which are historically important in the development of literature or of certain branches of literature which are to our purpose, but those in which the inner stresses and life of an age, 'its form and pressure,' are immediately present in the very texture of the words. And these texts are to be understood intuitively by the imagination and not discursively by the intelligence, concretely not abstractly, as literature not history.

The importance of an appreciative study of literature, music and the arts in fostering the growth of a religious attitude to life was never greater than today. We live in an age in which the strongest and most vocal opinion holds either explicitly or implicitly that man is essentially the passive product of his circumstances, and in which a reductive theory of explanation holds sway in nearly every department of thought. We live that is to say in an era which stresses what in man is conforming and accommodating. Such a view is antagonistic to a religious doctrine of man. But the whole validity of literature depends on seeing man as—in the last resort—a free and responsible person, as a tragic being and not merely as a sophisticated physical object. The arts and literature are handmaidens to religion because their system of assumptions belongs to the same order as the assumptions of the religious mind. If literature and the arts were cut out of the syllabus of the secondary school, the chances of understanding what Christianity is all about would be greatly reduced. And the *essentials* of an approach to them are the same whether we are dealing with the modern school child of twelve or a sixth former. The latter may be more intelligent and much more self-aware but his need to bring humility and unselfcentred understanding to his reading and listening and looking is as great. Teachers and pupils who study literature without a core of humility soon become lost in superficialities. Cynicism (sometimes the refuge of bright young critics) is little but an anti-rolling device for those spiritually at sea.

Much of what has been said about English literature is as true of literatures which may be studied in languages other than English; properly to understand another language asks for sensitiveness to its shades of meaning and to the ranges of feeling embodied in those meanings; and to translate demands a search among equivalences, a sympathy and a savouring of tone, of word and mood. Much of what has been said has, too, its relevance to music, architecture, painting, sculpture as much as to poetry, drama or prose, whether in the mother tongue or in a foreign language.

So far, however, we have not emphasized enough the importance to the child's life of creative work, whether in words, notes of music, craft or paint. In fact, for most children expression goes hand in hand with appreciation. Unless he writes, or sings or plays music, or composes, or paints himself, his understanding of what others have written or composed or painted will be shrivelled and limited. Making a poem or an essay or a carving may well have the fertilising effect upon a child's apprehension which doing an experiment or a piece of research may have for the scientist. To be able only to look upon oneself as an appreciator, never as a creator, is to fail, at any rate to some degree, to realize one's humanity. In creation there is a training in taking responsibility which can be of immense power.

Both for more and for less intelligent boys and girls work in the Art Room can add much to the meaning of life, enabling kinds of insight which otherwise might never develop. No doubt for the less intelligent child pottery may often be more suitable as an educative craft than the more exactingly accurate and 'intellectual' woodwork. But for many intelligent children too pottery has felt experiences to give that are of great value.

'In good art work,' says John Melser, 'or in musical composition, or movement, in drama or in story-writing, the teacher is requesting each child to record a personal reaction to some aspect of his own world and, on terms of equality, is welcoming that reaction as something new and important, as a statement which contributes to his, as well as the child's, understanding. The relationship between teacher and child is very different in this situation. They are two sharers in the common human predicament accepting together a statement symbolic of their experience and, whereas in the other case the relationship is 'formal', 'closed,' and based inevitably on the superiority of the one and the inadequacy of the other, in creative work there are open and exciting possibilities of mutual interaction growing out of the acceptance of and acquiescence in each other's nature. There is a 'personal encounter' between teacher and taught which results in a disinterested affection, an acceptance, and recognition, which is the essential preliminary to a proper education of feeling. This is not a mystical or even a particularly mysterious thing—the kind of fellow-feeling of which it is a species is as simple and spontaneous as the exchange between strangers of a commiserating grimace in a dull lecture.'

It is in shaping and creating things themselves, from whatever material, that some children may learn most really two related qualities which are perhaps essential to living a Christian life: humility and receptiveness. The same two qualities are needed for good personal relationships.

If a teacher gives a young child plenty of time and opportunity for experimental play with sand, water, clay, textiles, wood, bricks and stones, the child learns the essential nature of a material by feeling it on his skin and in his muscles, by experiencing its texture, its resistance or its malleableness. This play demands absence of tension and complete relaxation; the teacher's function is to provide a rich variety of materials and to create the right social climate, an atmosphere of warmth and tranquillity, in which a child can explore to the full the possibilities of the materials of his play. This is a not unChristian task. Whether he works in clay or wood or glass or metal, a craftsman can only achieve good work when the conditions of humility and receptiveness operate. He must subdue himself to the nature of the material in which he works and to the nature of the tools with which he works. He must respect both material and tool, demanding nothing alien of either. He accepts with voluntary submission their discipline, holding chisel or brush or saw as it demands to be held, using is so that its nature is fulfilled. The material must not be tortured into alien shapes. Form must be organic to material. It is when a preconceived pattern is imposed that an alien shape is forced on to the material. A feverish desire for self-expression, a self-concerned over-anxiety, may produce inability to perceive and to respond. In quiet relaxation, in the meeting of man and material, the material is able to convey to man how the play between them should culminate. The potter is involved with his clay and yet disinterested. He is absorbed and yet in detachment abstains from forcing a preconceived design upon it. This does not mean that he does nothing.

The same thing is true in the field of personal relationships. Detachment is not a deliberate selfish isolation from people but a sitting loose to the human situation. It is an absence of the tension which may arise when one is self-concernedly involved. It is not the neutrality or indifference of a spectator watching a struggle whose outcome does not concern him personally. The kind of detachment of which we are speaking is full participation, together with a willingness to leave things open and unfinished. It is the ability to be absorbed in the demands of the present without being disturbed at what cannot be done, or at what fails to develop as one hoped. This readiness to leave situations open seems to depend upon a conviction that there is a pattern and design, a harmony and order of which one is only partially aware. It depends too upon an acceptance of human limitations, one's own and other people's, an acknowledgement of human liability to error and blindness and of the incompleteness of all human insight and understanding.

Anything less than total involvement seems to indicate some degree of insincerity and self-centredness as fatal in the arts as in friendship and in religion. A surrender to the situation is the only real response that can be made. It may be response to a material, to a poem or a play or to music, as in the arts. It may be in response to a person or, for a teacher, to a group of children. It may be response to the liturgy, the collective prayer of the Christian community, or response in solitude to the Spirit of God. Each demands an emptying of self, a giving in singleness of mind. This living wholly in the situation is an aspect of integrity, a response to whatever the present demands without losing sight of the pattern, the purpose of a life as a whole. Detachment is not a denial of the need for effort. It does not mean sitting back in negligence leaving all activity to the Spirit of God. But it does necessitate a deliberate abstention from any attempt to manoeuvre the outcome for personal advantage. It comes when there is complete absorption and a total unawareness of self. Teachers rightly measure the success of their teaching partly at least by their ability to produce an absorption in which the children are drawn out of themselves.

The headmaster who wrote the Ministry of Education's pamphlet *The Story of a School* describes the long search made by himself and his staff for the activity which would produce absorption of the quality and intensity that they wanted. They found it eventually in free expressive movement, 'not movement which makes us feel we want to say something, which is Drama, not movement for developing bodily strength or skills, which is Physical Training, but movement for movement's sake, which is the starting point of all the arts.' He describes their failure with puppets, with speech training, with choral speech, with mimes and country dancing. It was only when the children were completely relaxed in free movement that they were also wholly absorbed, totally free of self-consciousness. The curriculum should give many such opportunities for obliviousness of self.

Much of what has been said of relations with the materials of the arts and of intra-personal relations is true of the Christian life. Without quiet relaxed receptiveness men are unable to respond to the formative power of the Spirit. But a desire to predetermine or to dictate the form which life shall take seems to produce rigidity and formalism. More is done when there is a quiet re-directing of the attention, and even that may suggest too positive an action.

CHAPTER FIVE

On Teaching History

(with a note on Social Sciences)

I

LIKE SCIENCE, history has inevitably much to do with facts. The method of modern historical scholarship is scientific in the sense that historians use a number of techniques which they claim are capable of establishing beyond reasonable doubt certain types of 'fact'—the authenticity or forgery of a document, the date of a building, the site of a battle—and which they assume will commend themselves as a basis for acceptance to others also trained to base conclusions on scientific evidence. But most people agree that historical interpretation goes beyond these techniques, that history is not concerned merely with the movement of bodies from one place to another but with the human motives which call forth those movements. The motives of men cannot be discovered by the application of techniques; our study of them is based upon our own accumulated and accumulating experience of human nature. But the more we study history, the more often we are brought up against 'facts' that do not square with the interpretation of character which we have constructed, so that one of two things has then to happen: either we go back and look again until we can, by external techniques, prove our previous fact to be wrong; or we take this awkward fact into our assessment of motive and achieve a more complex understanding of human character. Thus the study of history is a two-way traffic: we bring to it as our yard-stick our own knowledge of human nature, but we draw from it a deeper knowledge of the intricate realities of human persons.

This method is, in some sense, used by all who handle history today, and is common to Christian and non-Christian teachers. Is it enough for the Christian teacher? It is, as it were, a horizontal method in that its analysis is always of cause and effect on the horizontal line of time and that it applies no criterion from outside time, for it makes no acknowledgement of—still less claims to understand—a divine plan in history. It only deals with men's responses, not with that to which they respond. Thus, though a Christian writer and teacher of history *believes* that there is a 'vertical' understanding of history, that its reality is to be found in the impingement of God from outside time upon it, he *practises* an entirely horizontal interpretation. Here lies his dilemma. Though the Christian teacher is likely to believe that the development of historical scholarship during the last centuries has been a work of the human mind under God's guidance and that it has been an immense gain to learn how to know men and their institutions more truly, in more exact proportions with as little enhancement or distortion as possible, he must not arrogate to himself any special power of interpreting divine action in history, of pointing out the vertical meaning of history. The calling of the historian is not that of the prophet. But the Christian's conviction about the true nature of history does impinge very closely on his historical method at one point: it radically affects his view of human nature, which is the real criterion by which he makes historical judgments. He believes that everywhere in history Man is confronted by God and that ultimately history consists of Man's choice or rejection of God. However much the historical situation he analyses is built up of given circumstances, factors of heredity, environment, contingent event, however much, that is, choice is circumscribed by a real historic situation which it is his work to delineate, there remains for the Christian at the core of every such situation a real, unpredictable, in some sense unmeasurable, choice. The duty of the Christian historian lies in acknowledging this reality. He must make clear in his teaching his conviction that there is this element of spiritual choice embodied in all history, whether officially classified as secular or as ecclesiastical. He must, however, present this, not as a conclusion to be proved by the methods of historical study, but as a conviction about the 'stuff' of history which is brought *to* it, a conviction which is therefore open to challenge and which must be acknowledged as one among several possible ways of interpreting history.

He must also acknowledge his sense of the mystery implicit in all history, his awareness of the unknown quantity X which is the action of God impinging on all the events he analyses. Without claiming to include X in his analysis, he must acknowledge its presence and recognize that ultimately history cannot be completely analysed and 'taped' by methods of modern scholarship. One of the sins of modern historians is the arrogance of their claims that history is completely knowable, that the last word can be spoken about people, that their deepest secrets are susceptible to our analysis and that they are completely in our power. Against this the Christian can preach a true agnosticism, can refuse this assumption of power over people who to him are alive, not dead, can impart to his teaching an insistent note of humility and open-mindedness in face of mystery. He will, however, see in the study of history, both for his pupils and for himself, a means whereby we may grow in the understanding of men and the spiritual choices before them. Whilst training in analysis must play its part, he will attend as much to the training of the imagination, for it is sensitivity to new impressions and capacity for sympathetic understanding that he will most wish to encourage.

It is, then, with history as concerned with persons that

the Christian teacher should deal. Here he meets a considerable difficulty, for 'school' history, dominated as it tends to be by examination requirements and by the 'line of time' tradition, tends to be all but exclusively political or economic, and therefore impersonal and materialistic. This concentration on material things makes it difficult to introduce and foster a Christian outlook. Again, it often happens that the periods chiefly studied, at least in the upper forms of the grammar school, are the modern periods from the end of the seventeenth century to the beginning of the twentieth, with religious matters entirely or largely excluded from political considerations. This is likely to suggest to the pupil that what is not strictly political is of no public importance and that religion is a matter of purely private interest—not really the concern of the historian at all. Here again the 'line of time' method of teaching seems likely to exclude religious considerations. It is also to be noted that most history teaching tends to concentrate on a rather generalised 'common man' and to confine the common man's interest to the things which he can see and handle. This, however, is untrue to life and reality.

There is great need for more emphasis on the *individual* man and his personal response to the situations, human, political and moral, which confront him, the choice of courses of action which he makes. Christian teachers—and indeed all good teachers of history, whether Christian or non-Christian—will as far as they can select their material on this personal and individual basis.

In early adolescence, children tend to see people as absolutely black or white, right or wrong, good or bad; they identify themselves with the cause, or the hero, who happens to appeal to them; and they tend to accept their teacher's judgments. History teaching at this stage can hardly help being indoctrination. Whether it means to or not, it gives boys and girls certain personal heroes and certain group loyalties. Some children will never mature beyond this stage, but others, especially those who go on to sixth form courses, should be able to do so. What can the Christian teacher do about all this?

He can, in the earlier stages, introduce children to plenty of historical situations in which they can identify themselves with good men, whether Christian or not. He can show the qualities they possessed which moved them to behave as they did. He can go on to show that people, and certainly groups of people, even if they are predominantly 'good', are capable of 'bad' things, that their motives are mixed, sometimes noble, sometimes less than noble, even ignoble, partly black and partly white, just as the children are, and know they are, themselves. Here is an approach to a true knowledge of real people and of real human situations, an introduction to the real world of mixed motives and variegated characters. In this way, history teaching can be about human nature, it can be realistic, and it can show that goodness, right choices and high motives *matter* both to the individual and to the course of history.

In the later, more mature, stages something more is needed. This is an age when it is especially important to foster intellectual integrity based on critical judgment. One important element in history teaching in the fifth and sixth forms is to help pupils to realise that, as C. P. Scott taught, 'comment is free, but fact is sacred', and to teach them how to separate comment and fact. They need to achieve, as far as may be possible, the difficult feat of seeing how things look from the other side, to develop the imaginative sympathy to see both sides of a case passionately and clearly. This striving to see both sides of a case, and to try to recognize as accurately as possible the motives, personalities, philosophies and beliefs of real and individual people must necessarily involve at least the recognition of religious, and hence of Christian, elements in history. To neglect these is indeed to be culpably biassed, and to reckon without all the facts.

The personality, philosophy and belief of the teacher, whether he is a Christian or not, is bound to affect his teaching and the pattern of history which his pupils will be likely to see emerging from their study of the subject. In the study of the history of the Old Testament and of the New Testament the pattern is clear, and it is—without any possibility of misunderstanding—a religious pattern. There is no comparable pattern, clearly and unmistakeably set down in an accepted canonical form, for modern history. Indeed, the course of economic and political history, such as that of the Industrial Revolution, for instance, is only too likely to suggest a Marxist, and purely materialistic, pattern.

Though judgment in history belongs to God and the Christian teacher dare not assume the role of judge, neither dare he be indifferent, or appear to his pupils to be indifferent, to the great issues of good and evil in man's past. To imply that there is always equal right on both sides, to turn aside moral assessments on the ground that everything is relative to the standard of the age, this is to deny the seriousness of the issues we study. Whilst teaching the Christian duty of seeking to understand as fully as possible, we must also go on to demand of our pupils a full moral response to the situations they study.

One of the final lessons of history is that Man is on the move; that human nature is not changeless; that what is perennial—and unique—is the spirit of man; and that this spirit can show, and historically does show, a reaching out to something higher, to the 'good life'. Man's successes may be intermittent and limited, his follies and failures may be recurrent and often disastrous, but his spirit is unquenchable. He may be in his infancy, but at his best he already has a dignity and grace which point to the divine within him.

II

The approach to history in the secondary modern school is often made indirectly through social studies, but, whether this is so or not, social studies is a subject giving many opportunities for dealing with matters of importance and relevance. Included within its bounds may be not only history ('tracing history backwards') but geography, civics, architecture and ethics. All of these have a descriptive, factual content but they are human studies too. Geography —seen as the subject which deals with the physical, climatological and economic conditions under which communities live, and with relationships between communities in all parts of the world—is even more obviously concerned than is history with the recognition of the differences between races and peoples and the human problems which arise from them. While history is the study which can endow a man with a longer memory, the memory of his nation and civilization, geography is the study which can bring him to consciousness of other factors also determining her future. Professor Fleure was fond of saying to his students at Manchester, 'Society is older than man.' The individual is made what he is in great measure by social and geographical realities.

The child taught geography by a Christian teacher learns to accept those realities and to appreciate some of the inequality in physical endowment between nations and to understand their differences of need. It is a study which demands imagination, which can develop a sense of the indomitable spirit of man, and which to older pupils at any rate can illumine the difficulties presented to the makers of peace treaties by physical and economic considerations. In much teaching of geography there ought to be a greater recognition of the moral choices which have been or are involved in this development or that. Learning about 'environments of difficulty' can be a real excitement to children, for here they see the nobility of men in their struggles with nature. Children of eleven or twelve are gripped by an account of how the Dutch have won their richest farmland from the North Sea; of the exploration of America westwards (not forgetting how the Mormons sowed crops in the spring before leaving an area for one further west, with their fellows in mind who would later in the year be arriving there and reaping the harvest); and of the campaign continuing still year after year against disease in tropical Africa.

But whatever is taught in history or geography, or in social studies more generally, it is necessary not to gloss over man's inhumanity to man, or to hide the truth that there are some moral battles which seem to have been lost not won; and the failure of the sense of responsibility both of people in power and of ordinary folk. The fact of human sin is not to be gainsaid, and opportunity will arise for suggesting that the guilt is not attributable to other people only but lies deep in ourselves too. Nor does it belong simply to the past; it still persists. 'The Government', 'employers', 'Trades Unions', 'they' all may be blameworthy, but so are we. One of the dangers in teaching social history is the suggestion, apt to be unnoticeably embedded in what we say, that progress is more or less inevitable. Man has not really to do anything that is spiritually costly about it. There is a corresponding danger in teaching civics—the embedded suggestion that welfare and social justice have been 'arranged' or can be 'arranged' without effort or cost to anybody and that we ourselves are not involved in the least,

Problems of the fair wage, of the colour bar, of religious toleration, of the right of the individual to be treated fairly by the State, are highly discussable, but the Christian teacher can hardly be content if he has not quietly been able at some point to get over to at any rate some of his pupils that these are not problems to be settled by law alone, they involve moral decisions both by ourselves and by the law-makers on our behalf. There is no settling with a moral dilemma simply by cutting it dead.

In teaching any of the social studies, more use might well be made of biography. We have already suggested that some re-emphasis on the part played by persons in history is an important task for a Christian teacher of the subject. But greater emphasis on the personal element is important in teaching other social studies too. In geography or civics or current events it is the effort of the individual to dis-cover or achieve which often makes clearest the essential point of a lesson. Captain Cook, Albert Schweitzer, Winston Churchill, Ernest Bevin, Trevor Huddleston are examples. Nor need references to individual lives be a deceptive way of dealing with a general movement if certain precautions are taken. For the outstanding individual is often a man who is waging more obviously—whether he does it victor-iously or not—a warfare which is going on in many of his contemporaries.

CHAPTER SIX

The Teaching of Religious Knowledge Today

MANY SCHOOLS limit their teaching of religious knowledge to biblical history, the history of the church and the main tenets of Christian doctrine, any attempt to convey the spirit, meaning and power of religion being regarded as outside their province. But this is rather like contenting oneself with confining sexual education to biological descriptions, or the kind of approach to the teaching of literature which treats it as an intellectual discipline rather than, as was said earlier, an expression through words of complex human experience, having emotional as well as intellectual content. Certainly it is not the function of the teaching of scripture in the school to convert people to Christianity; but it must seek through the years to present what the central teachings and message of the New Testament really are. It must not therefore be content to suggest that the prophets and Christ himself were just interesting historical characters or ethical teachers—for that would be untrue. In addition it must try to get over their deep concern with the relationship of men to a God, and the Christian conception of God as a loving Father of men. The predominant emphasis should be on God as unchangeable rather than on the development of man's ideas of God through the ages.

Though this will not involve preaching or emotional teaching, the assumptions, beliefs, personality and background of the teacher will obviously matter greatly. The teacher of religious knowledge who does not understand what religion is really about can no more teach the subject than a teacher of art little moved by beauty can in any real sense of the term teach art.

In our schools we must have something to give to those children who afterwards may not become committed Christians. They too must be given a chance to see what Christianity is about, the kind of moral behaviour which it advocates and its idea that such behaviour is right because the nature of God is what it is. Though it may indeed be, generally speaking, the function of the school to get children to the point where the teaching of the church can begin to have a real meaning, the school's approach should open up new vistas and be a help to children to come to terms with the totality of life. It must be a subject which often challenges convention and the habit of 'getting by' with a merely non-committal outlook.

But there is nothing in this to prevent religious knowledge from being a subject with its own astringency and discipline. The teaching of scripture must, as far as possible, be placed intellectually on the same level as that of other subjects in the curriculum. And to study it, even for those brought up in Christian homes, should be a cure for that familiar modern dilemma of knowing that we are Christian in our hearts but not being sure what we are in our heads. The lack of well-qualified teachers is likely only too often to make the informed study of the Bible difficult. But even where the specialist is available there are still dangers to guard against. The competent scholar may not necessarily have the quality of personality to draw boys and girls by example to the faith which he expounds; it is undesirable to identify a competent knowledge of the scriptures too narrowly with one or two specialists, so that the scriptures become departmentalised and regarded as of as little concern to other specialists as, say, physical education may be to the teacher of history. Each school must solve as best it can its own problems of scripture teaching and of the best deployment of its teaching resources. But on the one hand lack of informed acquaintance with the scriptures should not leave its pupils ready to accept uncritically as Christian any and every attempt to translate central doctrines of the faith into a modern idiom. On the other, stumbling blocks must not be placed in the way of intelligent boys and girls by the ignorant identification of Christianity with long outmoded views on such matters as the relation between religion and science.

There is much to be said in favour of examinations in religious knowledge, including, at least in the case of grammar schools, external examinations. The subject must never be a soft option and schools which offer it in examinations do undoubtedly tend to treat it more seriously than those which do not. There is still great unwillingness on the part of boys and girls in many grammar schools to concentrate seriously, at any rate up to 'O' level, on other than their examination subjects. It is perhaps significant that far fewer boys than girls at present offer Scripture in an external examination—particularly at 'A' level. In two recent years taken together, for example, the total number of boys offering Scripture at 'A' level in four of the largest examining boards' examinations was 280, the corresponding number of girls being 963.[1] Admittedly the syllabuses in some G.C.E. scripture examinations at both 'O' and 'A' level are so narrow in their understanding of the scope of the subject —factual and almost without challenge to thought—that they are perhaps better avoided. But others give an opportunity for imaginative, wide-ranging yet scholarly teaching and learning, though in all more questions might profitably be set of a philosophical or ethical type.

[1] 1954 and 1955. London General Schools; Cambridge Local; N.U.J.M.B.; Welsh Joint Board.

In days such as these the scripture teacher likely to be most successful in religious education is one who without sacrifice of integrity can manage to keep at not too great a 'distance' from his or her pupils. In teaching an understanding of the Bible, as in the discussion of problems of ethics or conduct, it is wisest to suggest, as occasion allows, that adults are just as much travelling along a road as their pupils. In a school where discipline in general stems from mutual respect and not from unquestioning obedience to 'authority', this is not impossible to do. They should be helped to see that there are for us no cut-and-dried, final answers, and that any man, Christian or non-Christian, who is prepared to be smug about his position should be suspect. Most adolescents pass through a stage where they like neat answers and for that reason some boys and girls are likely to leave school 'confirmed' agnostics or 'fundamentalist' Christians.

The psychology of adolescent commitment needs to be worked out. In some a vivid experience, necessarily partial, inhibits further spiritual development, leading to bigotry or to disillusion. In others, apparently the same experience, no less partial, is a gateway to growth. It is obvious that the insights of the mature cannot be grafted on to the young; they have their own journey to make from their own starting point. For them, to be open to growth is to be alive, to know the 'right' answers may be to die. It is well to bear in mind Simone Weil's sentence: 'One must be wholly prepared to abandon religion, even though that means abandoning all reason for living, if it be anything but the truth.'

It is at this point that something must be said about the renewed and growing appeal which fundamentalism has. Whenever a group of teachers, clergy and others actively concerned about religious education reaches the point of discussion of difficulties and difficult pupils, the humanist, the materialist, the indifferent and the merely stupid are discussed with reasonably constructive cheerfulness. The pupil about whom desperation and a sense of helplessness is expressed is one convinced that he is of the few 'true Christians,' as his teacher is not. He and his kind complain that in scripture lessons 'the unity of the Bible is handled frivolously,' they warn others off 'bad dangerous books' (by, for example, T. W. Manson or C. H. Dodd) on the library shelves. Convinced that they are 'saved', and this means something very real, they have been taught that since Christ lives in them they can do no wrong and are above criticism. They create a real cleavage between the pious and the thoughtful in a sixth form and permit the latter to reject religion with a fairly clear conscience.

The fact is that while the little child, and the mature adult who has become as a little child, no longer want to put their fingers in the prints of the nails, when they can say 'My Lord and my God', the adolescent sixth former who is basically unsure of his allegiance demands such premature, concrete satisfaction. An infallible book and, more important, a few infallible adults who are hero-worshipped and who interpret this book for them give immediate satisfaction, though often at the price of arresting growth.

In this situation not all of our scripture teaching is imaginative or helpful enough. Many who teach it, and more who draw up syllabuses, belong to the generation for whom fundamentalism was an old bondage from which they were glad to be released. The fundamentalism of schoolchildren is a new protective armour they have assumed voluntarily—for very few have parents of similar persuasion, most of them are the children of agnostic or indifferent parents, and many return to their parents' indifference when enthusiasm wanes.

Emphases in Bible teaching that were liberating and

illuminating against a background of fundamentalism and conservatism are confusing or merely dull against a background of unbelief. It is no longer exciting to hear how the Bible is a book like other books, but it is exciting to hear how it is unique. To hear for example the plagues of Egypt explained as natural phenomena is boring, or frankly alarming, unless accompanied or preceded by the assurance that Christians do believe in miracle and in the reality of the spiritual world. This is not to suggest that our teaching should simply give children what they want or that it should not disturb them; but that a more imaginative sympathy with their uncertainties is called for.

One cannot, whether trusted or not, turn people from fundamentalism or near-fundamentalism by a frontal attack, but its power can be sapped and its worst consequences mitigated by teaching in the ordinary course of school to nourish the life of the imagination. T. S. Eliot and George Herbert can act as powerful liberators. The really important things to be remembered are that one may dislike and distrust fundamentalism, but love most fundamentalists and that one must never say or think of their activities, 'This is going too far, this is being too religious,' but 'This is not religious enough. This in fact, in its cosy individualism, denies the Lordship of Christ over the whole of life.' And it is here that we have to part company with humanist colleagues, with whom of course in deploring many of the results of obscurantism we have been in close agreement.

The Christian life is essentially one of movement—a branch of dynamics and not statics. Flux is normal and necessary: what matters is the direction of the arrow. This is true of individual growth and of the church's life in the world. Definitions and systematisations require balance, equilibrium, delimitation, finality; in experience it is unbalance, paradox, tension, movement that constitute life, which is constantly a-dying and being born again. To fix may mean to fixate—the difference between orthodoxy and traditionalism.

There are many diverse experiences within the Christian tradition that any one man can know for himself. Two of the dangers in teaching scripture are these: to regard our own experience as defining Christianity, to call our own best understanding 'the truth'—this is the danger of sectarianism or sectionalism; and to become so charitably catholic, so wide in our sympathies, that conviction degenerates into an easy complacency and we lose ourselves. In some way— by the exercise of an enquiring mind coupled with humility, by disinterestedness coupled with a strong pastoral concern —we have to keep alive ourselves and allow our pupils to be themselves, always 'respectful of their growth towards personality.'

Two facts have to be put together, and our pupils are often aware only of the first. One is that religious men of equal distinction and integrity in different parts of the world think differently in a way not found, for example, among experts in science. The other, in the words of M. V. C. Jeffreys, is that 'the Christian revelation is alone commensurate with the full dimensions of life.'

One of the difficulties in the Christian teaching of scripture, as we have already hinted, is for the schoolmaster to possess, in right proportion and kind, both detachment and committal. To be fully human is necessarily to live committedly. The good scientist, the good historian and the good philosopher are deeply loyal members of appropriate groups, groups which have values and commitments of particular sorts. The good man or Christian—who may of course also be a scientist or historian or philosopher—is more widely and deeply committed still, and whatever subject he teaches he will remain a human being loyal to his presuppositions, faith and beliefs. There can be no escape, if a man is sincere, from the individual responsibility of being the individual he is. Neither will he forget that statements objectively true can still be false to the intensity of our experience of what they say; and that to pretend otherwise is to be insincere. But if he is to teach well, he will often need, though he is basically committed and not concealing the fact, to be genuinely detached and neutral 'on top' in his function as an intelligent, disciplined instructor and guide. And this is particularly necessary at the sixth form stage.

Even a lesson on belief in God meant for a sixth form should seek for no particular sort of response, and precautions should be taken lest it appear that privacy is being invaded. A compulsory class is not a voluntary church group; the teacher is not a preacher.

The core of the scripture syllabus throughout the school must be the central teaching of the Bible itself. Parts of that may well, if they are really seen, be disturbing and unpalatable to the present-day mind—the fact of the crucifixion and the reality of sin, for example. The idea that the greatest single event in human history is already over is also one that does not readily appeal, for the notion that the real past is that which is always present is a difficult and alien one to young dwellers in the twentieth century. Evolution, as Eliot says, easily becomes

> 'in the popular mind
> a means of disowning the past.'[1]

The more closely a teacher of scripture knows his boys or girls the more effective his teaching is likely to be. 'I did not get to know the children nearly well enough,' is a frequent cause of failure in teaching the subject. Certainly the

[1] *The Dry Salvages*, II.

more closely one is in touch with one's pupils the easier it will be to get the necessary 'level of detachment' right, for that is closely related to an understanding of their needs both as permanent human beings and as human beings who are very contemporary—more contemporary indeed than the teacher may always be able to be himself.

CHAPTER SEVEN

Worship in the School

I

INSTRUCTION perhaps does not require a community; corporate worship is impossible without one. It is necessary to ask, however, in what sense a school—and especially a maintained school—can be a Christian community. Many members of its staff will probably not be overtly Christian and many of its pupils will come to it day by day from homes which are products of the age. But many of the essential problems even of schools on a religious foundation, maybe with a chapel of their own, are not basically as different from those of the rest as might be supposed.

A school is a compulsory society. Does this mean that it cannot ever properly be regarded as a Christian society? Many of the characteristics, after all, which make it a true community are themselves characteristics of a Christian society, but at the least its compulsory nature must limit the extent to which a school can be regarded as one. A careful look at these limitations may help us: some of them are general limitations affecting any school at any period, others are particular limitations especially applying to our twentieth century position.

The general limitations are of two kinds—those that spring from the fact that a school is a hierarchical community of adults on the one hand and boys and girls on the other; and those which spring from the fact that their attendance is compulsory. Because it is a hierarchical society it is one governed by law. In such a society as a school it would not do, at least for school purposes, to treat the prodigal pupil as the parable does treat the prodigal son. The law-abiding brother must be supported. The principle on which the labourers in the vineyard were paid is not really applicable in the field of class management. A school, like a state, is a mixed community and must live by the rules of natural justice. The morality of grace is something that must be freely offered; it cannot be imposed. But there is another kind of limitation which is also important—a limitation on the extent to which a school can express itself in worship. Prayer must not be used as an aid to discipline. The avoidance of litter is something that may be very important in the life of a school at a particular time, but it is not something which can be prayed about in assembly because, though such a prayer might be sincere enough in all conscience as far as the staff is concerned, it could hardly be expected to be so for the pupils. The number of things which can reasonably and legitimately be made the subject of school prayer is smaller than the number of objects which can reasonably be regarded as matters of school policy.

The other general limitation which springs from the fact that a school is a compulsory community is that it is bound to contain non-Christians as well as Christians—and some of the former may be better and morally more mature than some of the latter. Clearly parents have rights—and more than the legal safeguards of an Act of Parliament. Boys and girls have their rights too. Their opinions, their attitudes, must be respected: it is a Christian duty to respect them. They ought not to be forced into hypocrisy. Attraction is the only legitimate magnet. This delicacy in approach has always been necessary (though not always practised), but it is perhaps especially needed today so that it almost merges into the second sort of limitations, those which are characteristic of the twentieth century.

The most obvious contemporary limitation to the school

as a Christian community is that it has to serve several competing versions of what a Christian society is. A voluntary school in the world of maintained schools, or an independent school outside it, can avoid some of the embarrassments of the situation. In them there can be a true relation between the pupil as a member of his school community and as a member of the Christian community; a relation which can never perhaps be so free or satisfactory in the world of county schools. But yet in another sense the pupil, and still more the teacher, in a county school is in a better position to see the true facts of the Christian world as it is. The Christian teacher and the Christian pupil in a church school need not be bothered, if they don't want to be, by the divisions of Christendom. Their school and their church can be ivory towers, though, of course, there is no reason why they should be. The Christian teacher and the Christian pupil in a county school have no such retreat. Is it better to face the facts? Almost certainly it is for the teacher, but the pupil's case is somewhat different. Swimming is not learned in the deep end—and Christian division can be pretty bad when seen from a county school.

The most obvious differences, however, which mark our contemporary climate of opinion are not those which lie between the various denominations, but those which lie between Christians on the one hand and non-Christians on the other, leaving in the middle the bewildered majority of fellow-travellers who are not quite sure in which direction they are travelling.

Another contemporary limitation in a school as a Christian community, and an internal one this time, is that its teachers are not selected as Christians. Certainly religious tests are quite impossible politically in county schools, but one is tempted to ask whether they would not also be quite ineffective if they were allowed. We have clearly recognized

earlier in this book that school staff rooms will be mixed
societies, like the world at large, containing Christians and
different varieties of non-Christians. In some the balance
will be tipped in such a way that it would be quite unreal-
istic to talk of that school as a Christian community; in
others the staff will be predominantly Christian. But, as we
have seen, many of those who are very doubtful about a
number of Christian doctrines are quite clear about their
retention of the Christian ethic, and conspicuous in their
practice of it in their treatment of their pupils. They doubt
where they cannot believe; they do not oppose. They are
usually not unwilling that those with a fuller faith should
lead the school as a Christian community. On the contrary,
they often welcome it gladly. They themselves may never
go to church on Sundays but they 'rather like having a
church not to go to.'

A third contemporary limitation is the fact that at any
rate senior boys and girls are aware of the general climate
of opinion. Where so many adults doubt, they are often
unwilling to give more than a provisional adherence. A
group of clever fifth form boys in a public school were
debating the right age for confirmation. Some had been
confirmed at twelve, others had not yet been confirmed. All
were agreed on two things. They thought that, in so far
as confirmation was a condition of admission to communion,
they should have been confirmed before coming to their
public school; they wanted to live there as Christians, and
they felt they needed all the spiritual help they could be
given. They were also clear, however, that, in so far as
confirmation involved a personal permanent undertaking of
baptismal vows, they ought not to have been asked for
such a promise at their age in view of what they now knew
of the adult world and its opinions and practices. Though
perhaps only clever fourteen-year-olds would have formu-

lated their beliefs so clearly, we believe that their position would be widely endorsed by their contemporaries.

II

But if, in view of all these limitations, it may be difficult to regard a normal secondary school as in any unqualified sense a Christian community, it can nevertheless be truly a society many members of which learn a good deal about the nature of Christianity and the Christian life during their passage through the school. What in more practical terms does this mean?

The period of worship, whether, as usual, it is held at the beginning of every school morning or whether—as in some schools where numbers of children arrive late because of trams and bus timings—it is held later in the day, is one of the most powerful agents a school can use for helping children to apprehend what religion is about. The work of Lewin on attitude changes makes it clear that in a relatively open society sheer instruction, however attractive and accurate, is almost completely ineffective in modifying attitudes. There is of course an element of instruction in the daily assembly for worship. But its primary value lies in giving a new direction, even if temporarily, to the attention and intention of those taking part in it. The more deeply they take part the more potent its influence will be. The central task of education, as the Christian conceives it, is to give every child a chance to understand that his individual life, with the experiences pouring in upon it, has a meaning in God's eyes. The Christian hopes to make it possible for at any rate some children to have a 'still point' at the centre.

And yet, however reverent and impressive morning service in school may be, and however easily and successfully the 'secular' disabilities of the school hall in which it takes place may be overcome or forgotten, it is well to appreciate the difference between religious observance in a school and religious observance in a church in the point from which they start. The head of a school can assume greater mental alertness but less experience of life than the priest or minister. He cannot, as we have said, assume even an initial interest in worship on the part of many who come. To some of his colleagues on the platform religion will be wholly irrelevant to anything they find worthwhile. He has a wider cross section of public opinion in front of him than the parson. 'That is what you think, not what I think,' may be the unspoken comment on much that he says. 'Are you not taking for granted answers to philosophical questions which are still open?' Moreover, his 'congregation' has not come voluntarily for a religious exercise. Yet there is a common loyalty, a social solidarity, which rarely exists in a church. A church service without religious content would be empty; a school assembly without specifically religious content might yet be a valuable feature in the life of the school, an integrating experience. Further there is a sense in which attendance at a church is a withdrawal from the world, withdrawal and return being a usual alternation in the Christian life; but a school assembly is not a withdrawal from the life of a school—it is the place where its foundation principles can be made explicit and related to their source in God.

There are expressions of the Christian faith wholly suitable for a church service which are not suitable for a school assembly. In particular, should any of the prayers be addressed to Jesus Christ? 'I find it right and proper,' says one headmaster, 'to address prayers to God the Father and to God the Spirit; but this is the psalmists' faith. The nearer we get to the core of specifically Christian devotion the more hesitant I am about using it in assembly. It is as though with a miscellaneous audience religion must be more objective, less personal. Yet I do find myself at certain seasons of the year using "O Lord Christ, who didst set thy face as a flint to go to Jerusalem, . . ." I am jealous for the sincerity in worship of my uncommitted pupils and do not like using language ahead of their foreseeable range of experience.' Perhaps prayers should be made in the name of Christ—'through Jesus Christ our Lord'—rather than to him.

Certainly there must be consciousness in school prayers that the school is a community of human beings and that it is natural and right for a community to pray. To remember in a prayer those members of the community who are ill or undergoing stress—for example the stress of an external examination—is usual in some schools and such 'holding of others in God's presence' can have its effect on many who listen even though some of them as individuals may remain pretty detached.

It is essential that whatever prayers are in fact prayed and whatever lessons are in fact read should be seen to apply quite as much to the adult members of the community as to the boys and girls. It is far better to have a morning service which the children feel it to be difficult to understand than one which they know the adults will consider childish. 'The Headmaster of my last school,' wrote one of our correspondents, 'at the beginning of every school year read St. Paul's famous passage on Charity and prayed the appropriate collect. And before doing so he made it clear that this was primarily for himself and for the other members of the common room to remind them of the way they ought to behave towards the boys and each other, the way in which things ought to be done in the school. The seniors would understand a good deal of what was meant, and the juniors would understand a little more each year. Here was the crux of the Christian faith as it applies to action, and no member of the common room could possibly scoff at it. He would cut very little ice with the boys if he tried.'

Sheer sincerity will get through, defective in many ways though the leader of the worship may be and know himself to be. No man has ever really prayed or tried to pray without learning something worthwhile — and teaching something to others if they are his congregation. There is an 'intention' and a relaxation about prayer that can be profoundly educative. If a headmaster is not unfriendly to the Christian position and though a humanist at heart willing to go a long way with it, at least in his capacity as a headmaster, he may well be willing to entrust the taking of the morning service occasionally—perhaps even once or twice a week—to another, or others, on the staff whom he knows to be more convincedly Christian than he. It will be unfortunate if a Christian, or even a humanist, finds it impossible to delegate the taking of the service to anyone save his second-in-command if the latter is a fairly decided agnostic. How easy it is for the same sentences to be said as the head himself may use, but in a tone of such manifest unbelief that a whole anti-God gospel is preached through the words uttered!

Certainly the content of the morning service must seem to those who attend it to be relevant to their interests, concerns and needs. If, as in a number of schools, some of the prayers used are written by pupils, it will still be necessary for the head to approve them carefully with this principle in mind. It is in fact a good deal more difficult to educate through what a child feels to be irrelevant than is sometimes assumed : in that case the matter does not impinge, it is apt to seem dull and meaningless. 'Your share in it is what you make' is often true of a school service. But one must beware of assuming that only the popular, the schoolboyish, the school or public event, will be felt as relevant.

Many people are willing from time to time (not all the time) at a service to be more imaginatively serious and adult than is their normal 'attitude'. The sentimental and the jejune will nearly always be recognized by a proportion of a school congregation to be false—as indeed they are.

This is one reason why in school worship the hymns sung and the tunes they are sung to should be carefully chosen. Perhaps the hymns used should for the most part be fairly objective: 'How great the harvest is,' rather than the self-dramatising 'There is a fountain filled with blood,' nor perhaps the subjective 'Jesu, lover of my soul' unless the occasion is a service at which attendance is voluntary and meant for those sympathetic with the full Christian position.

What should be the relationship between religious worship and education in the school and the local church? There are two groups of pupils for which the answer should be given. Ideally the pupil with live church commitments should find the worship of the school unsatisfactory, or at any rate incomplete (though he may find its lessons stimulating). It is not that he should find a lack of sincerity or honesty; rather that his particular Christian devotion should go further than a school's can. And the pupil without any kind of Christian commitment should find a religious view of life intellectually respectable and school worship an enlarging thing. Its worship should take him to the church door.

School religion is essentially introductory. It is concerned primarily with the first large step from a secular to a religious attitude to life; it can only go a certain distance with the second step from a religious attitude to a fully Christian one. Yet it is more than peripheral to the Christian faith. It must not lay such claim on the hearts of its pupils that later they suffer from nostalgia for the school chapel or the worship they had at school day by day. Rather in that worship the boy or girl should have learnt standards of reticence and dignity, and worth in music and words, which will carry over to church work. There is always a tension between what is and what should be. One function of morning assembly is to establish the relevance of worship to the corporate life of the school as a felt fact and as an intellectually accepted fact. This accepted relevance should transfer to the outside world, itself creating a large part of that inner tension which characterises the adult, and which is productive in due time of social reform.

For many pupils the regular morning worship will be the only service they ever attend, at any rate after the age of thirteen or so when they become too big to go to Sunday school any more. And in some suburbs and parts of the country only a minority are likely ever to have been Sunday school members. The very regularity and taken-for-granted-ness of morning assembly can have its effect: for one of the primary duties of the school is the non-inhibition of faith, and civilization outside it in these days does tend to inhibit belief. But it is not only the regularity that will matter but the occasional moment when a word can find a home, when a symbol or a sentence is not only of use for getting into touch with truth but for getting into touch with power too.

There is a sense in which all Christian teaching and observance in a school remains unclinched—and only by a voluntary act on the part of the boy or girl can it be clinched. The seed can be sown, that is enough. Enlightenment rather than conversion, understanding rather than discipleship are the aims of a school, as a school, whether in the classroom where religious knowledge is taught or in the periods of worship it conducts.

In addition to their short daily services schools without chapels of their own often give opportunities on special occasions for corporate worship outside their regular routine

—in, for example, services for leavers, on saints' days or at end of term. Some have services periodically at the various neighbouring churches, in turn. Organized relations with the different branches of the Church must depend so much on local circumstances that it is not possible to generalise about them. But experience has certainly shown that school conferences of the Student Christian Movement sometimes provide a chance for bringing clergy and ministers of various denominations into touch with the boys and girls of the schools in their neighbourhood; and may even lead on to voluntary activities by these boys and girls in association with churches or a council of churches.

CHAPTER EIGHT

The Sixth Form

TWENTY YEARS ago the sixth form in many grammar schools contained between five per cent and ten per cent of the children in the school. Now the proportion may be twenty per cent and it is still going up. Whereas in 1938 13,200 candidates entered for some part of the Higher School Certificate examination, in 1958 77,505 candidates took one or more subjects in the corresponding G.C.E. examination (Advanced level). With the rapid expansion of the universities themselves, of technical colleges and colleges of advanced technology, and with the increasing level required for entering a training college, the number is likely to continue to rise even more sharply in the next ten years. The sixth form, particularly in maintained schools, is catering for a wider range of intelligence than it used to do. It is also catering for a considerably wider social range. An appreciable proportion of sixth formers in some areas have regular 'spare-time' jobs in out-of-school hours both during term-time and in holidays. To have money in one's pocket is an essential to the self-esteem of far more sixth formers than twenty years ago.

Perhaps we give too little attention to visualising what we really want our young people of eighteen to be like. Is liveliness as fundamental a virtue as the Americans believe? How important is a wide range of interest? the beginnings of a personal philosophy of life? a sense of social responsibility?

In some ways undoubtedly a sixth form should be a junior university—but it must be adapted to the needs of many not themselves going on to a university course afterwards and it must be far more interested in the individual than the university often tends to be. While, inevitably, much of the education of children below the sixth form stage is a matter of helping them to be 'dyed the colour of the best in their civilization'—though with increasing awareness on their part—now a strong effort must be made to develop their capacity for taking an external view. Yet at the same time they must be safeguarded from a belief that anyone can *live* in detachment. Neutrality is 'the pause between breathing out and breathing in,' not a substitute for breathing . . . or for action. After all, when it comes to making a decision the completely neutral, unbiassed person is reduced to choosing by the toss of a coin.

There seems a good deal of evidence to suggest that many sixth formers today are less speculatively minded than their predecessors of twenty years ago. They expect to be taught and are perhaps less inclined to think or read on their own. Some of this may be due to overloaded syllabuses and the amount of sheer memory-content demanded by A level examinations, but more of it in all probability to the temper of the world outside. During their two, or (for an increasing number) three, years in the sixth, boys and girls should come to see not only the importance of clear thinking—and thinking which is as objective as possible—but the challenge to speculation and to personal concern with at least a number of the big issues of our time. Many of these will not be seen as big issues if a habit of cold analysis has become too pervasive.

> 'The man who will not see
> Because he doth not feel'

is already known in sixth forms. Unless boys and girls have already at seventeen some inkling of the compelling power in life of love, beauty and religious belief, their values are likely to go easily awry. They may come to hold that there is only one kind of truth that is true, the sort yielded by detached observation; and they may well suffer in consequence from a barrenness of mind which is much in need of fertilization. Much inevitably will depend upon the spirit in which sixth form studies are carried on and upon their scope. It is still true, as Geoffrey Barraclough remarked some years ago, that far too much sixth form work has in fact no value apart from examinations. 'In the school we train for O and A, not for Alpha and Omega.'

Too narrow and rapid a course in a specialized field may permanently close many doors in the mind. There is truth in these remarks made by a committee recently interviewing candidates for university awards: 'Members of the Committee were shocked by the poor response of many of these highly-selected candidates, who found it difficult to speak clearly about their own particular interests, who showed surprising ignorance of, and indifference to, the affairs of the world and who for the most part showed no intellectual activity outside their speciality. "I have no time for reading" was a frequent remark.' Even abler sixth formers may come to substitute intellectual development for a development which involves them as people more completely. In this way they slip away from some of the challenges—moral, aesthetic, religious—which decidedly they ought to have to meet.

Nevertheless intellectual development—the development of the cool reason—is of very great importance. One aim of what are often called 'general studies' is to produce an enquiring mind. We are not primarily concerned to impart information, though we may do so in passing, but to train boys and girls in sensitive and coherent thinking. This training will include diverse but closely linked activities: the handling of evidence; the understanding of relevance; the understanding of rational thought according to the logical demands of the subject-matter (compare Aristotle's 'We must be content with so much precision in our statement as the subject before us admits of; for the same degree of accuracy is not to be expected in all kinds of reasoning'); knowledge of the limitations of any given method, and appreciation of the differences of method in various branches of knowledge; the enlargement of the critical faculties; the enlargement of sensibility; practice in clear exposition and the lucid presentation of points of view; passing from handling descriptive and concrete language to discursive and abstract language; the opportunity to be at close quarters with great minds at work; and becoming acquainted with moral, political, philosophical and religious ideas. It would not appear that a programme of this sort is as common as is sometimes imagined.

While General Studies should include Christian apologetics and reference to the Christian faith, they must not be made primarily into an opportunity to defend the faith or to persuade pupils to become committed Christians. This, however, precludes neither the honest expression of one's own views nor the removal of such barriers as may perhaps prevent pupils from believing. Critical doubt has a great part to play in the formation of an enquiring mind, and the asking of radical questions which lay open the presuppositions of belief is an important part of a pupil's training through General Studies.

General Studies, however well they are taught, are unlikely to be enough in themselves to produce people who are not merely cultured and enlightened, but Christian. Much more will depend as far as this latter task is concerned on the spirit of the school and particularly upon the personal influence of sixth form masters and mistresses. The dominant tradition in English grammar school education is really far more concerned with producing balanced, temperate and knowledgeable gentlemen than Christians. What one of our correspondents says about the classical curriculum is almost as true of some others: 'Although there is much in it that is favourable to Christianity, it is possible for the opposite result to happen. The toughness of the subject seems to me to have an effect on the minds of those who undergo it; they tend to emerge mentally "hard-boiled". By this I mean that the classicist (formed or being educated) is apt to be ruthless in his opinions and sceptical in his judgments. Though this does not necessarily imply an anti-Christian or even an unChristian attitude, it often happens that boys do develop intransigent views of that sort. This means that any master, but particularly a Christian, needs to be honest and equally tough in his own opinions and judgment to earn the respect of his boys, be they Christian or not.'

General Studies which are too completely exercises of the intelligence and concentrate too exclusively on increasing knowledge and developing the powers of reason may do little to develop that maturity of heart-with-mind which the Christian would like to see. A boy with an amazing power of comprehension may have much less power of apprehension. Able severely to discipline his mind to accept only what is 'evidence' he may remain arrestedly adolescent of soul and fitted to share that sad reflection of Kingsley Amis's Lucky Jim that 'he knew absolutely nothing whatsoever about other *people* and their lives.'

An enquiry into the views, interests and activities of sixth form boys in six typical grammar schools conducted in 1958 by a headmaster in the North Midlands suggests that the amount of really discriminating reading outside the syllabus done by sixth formers may be startlingly small. About one pupil in seven among those questioned had read no books in his spare time from September, 1957 to February, 1958; the majority of books read were topical adventure, war stories or biographies—though at least half those questioned had time to visit the cinema regularly. 'Clearly,' comments the inquirer, 'it is more necessary than ever for sixth form teachers to advise and investigate general reading.'

But not merely to advise and investigate. Actual discussion, preferably in smallish groups, of ideas and notions derived from the reading is imperative. The groups will need to consist of people of about the same level of maturity (some boys and girls are, even intellectually, far more mature outside school than their school behaviour would appear to indicate). And, if staffing will permit, it is well for people to belong to two discussion groups of different sizes. In the teaching of Divinity to sixth forms a good deal of discussion is often encouraged—some of it arising from books set for reading perhaps. There is especially a temptation in this subject to have the groups too large, for arts and science sixths are combined for the Divinity class in many schools; and this sometimes means that only the more vociferous or less shy take much real part in the discussion and that too few in fact express views which have any personal depth.

Almost all our efforts with a sixth form will tend to be of less value if side by side with them we do not allow the pupil all the time we can for private study and leisure for his own intellectual pursuits. The greatest lovers of wisdom and beauty were also the greatest lovers of leisure; it was not for nothing that Heraclitus had all the time in the world to tire the sun with talking and send him down the sky.

But, all said and done, the most valuable part of many a sixth former's education comes from that many-dimensional taking of responsibility for others which falls to him. In a school which tries to give a Christian education as many sixth formers as possible will be given real responsibility for other children and given it in a way which involves human relationships. The prefect who is merely a functionary is not learning what he should be learning. There is need for sixth formers to do things *with* others lower in the school and not merely do things *to* them. In no other part of school life are the attitudes of teachers to taught more likely to be guides to the taught in their turn. A teacher can easily deprive a boy or girl of personality or not notice that he has one. The academic mind is subject to the temptation of assuming that you can usually get the answer to a question in terms of fact, whereas many answers can only be given in terms of men. Responsibility creates; and we often under-estimate the degree and depth of responsibility we can profitably give young people of seventeen or eighteen.

CHAPTER NINE

Outside the Time-Table[1]

THE QUALITY of the out-of-classroom activities of a school tends to be closely related to the quality of the personal relationships between staff and pupils. Often it is a few members of staff who make all the difference. But unless some at any rate are felt to be human beings, who bring a generous amount of their humanity to school, the chances are that few activities will develop spontaneously outside time-table hours. The example of the master or mistress who throws himself without self-interest into membership of the school dramatic society or scout troop or S.C.M. is very far reaching.

Much depends in education upon the level at which pupils trust the master or mistress. Personal trust is an antiseptic against temptations—including the temptation to waste leisure. 'Wasting one's substance in riotous living' means not simply wasting one's money, but wasting one's character too. This being said, however, it needs to be said also that in non-time-tabled hours as much freedom as possible should be allowed to children to choose which societies they shall have and which they shall join. A proviso may need to be made, in some schools at any rate, that no child is a member of more than, say, three clubs or 'activities' in any one term. If the idea of founding a particular society comes from a member of staff—as it often may—it should come from him as a person rather than as a teacher; and a good deal of the initiative for deciding the details of how it should be carried on must be left to the children.

[1] This chapter owes an especial debt to Miss C. B. Galton, Headmistress of Cranborne Chase School.

School societies are so important in helping maturity and independence to blossom that if for one reason or another they cannot meet after the school day is over, room may need to be made for them by lengthening the lunch hour or by arranging that the school day finishes altogether at 2.30 or 3.0 on one afternoon a week, though the children will not of course go home until the usual time. But obviously it is best if the meetings take place after normal school hours.

Schools differ very greatly in the range of societies and activities available in out-of-school hours; a large number have not only musical and craft activities, but plays, social service ventures, societies of the hobby type (stamp-collecting, photography, bird-watching, model railways) to say nothing of discussion and debating groups and societies addressed by speakers from outside the school. It would seem that the child must be more sided than is human if he is, over the terms, to take a full part in the programme provided for him. And there is a real danger that the very variety of the offerings in some schools may lead to dissipation of concern and shallowness. The same questions may be raised by the out-of-school activities as are posed by the sort of world outside the school altogether in which the child of the 1960's will find himself.

Has this multilateral child of today got a centre? Can he find it in the climate and conditions and among the people that our various types of schools provide? Can we feel happy and sure that we are in fact giving him the *experience* whereby he may be enabled to find for himself some guiding principles and ideals that will stand the test of time? In other words, is he finding out more and more, as the wood becomes less and less visible because of the trees, where and what the centre of his being and of the universe, his universe, really is?

Activities outside the time-table should perhaps be based on three principles: limitation, acceptance, experience. To-day there is perpetual danger of dissipation of energy and of knowledge. A frightening sense of the illimitableness as well as the limitlessness of the universe presses upon us—even when by scientific advance we seem increasingly to limit it. One of the ways of countering this tendency to distraction is by giving children a chance to get to grips with material that does submit to their will, that is susceptible of control, that does not by its very size and strangeness induce fear, or a sense of futility, but which gives confidence and a feeling of mastery. All forms of plastic art answer the purpose: modelling in clay, carving in stone or wood, pottery, work in metal, carpentry. Also, to some extent, painting—in fact, all such forms of creative activity as bring them into direct contact with material, whether pliable or recalcitrant, which take time to make, which result in objects that are not primarily utilitarian (though these have their place); which give opportunity for the bold, large object or for the painstakingly detailed one. A wide range of choice is important, provided that dilettante approach is sternly discouraged. Though at first the child may make many mistakes, as he grapples with his medium he will learn to accept 'misfires' as part of the discipline of the artist or craftsman. And, if he moves on at all in creative fields of this kind, he may experience the inward dissatisfaction of the true artist. He will also learn to recognize and to respect fine and careful craftsmanship when he meets it and, under expert guidance, may begin to develop some standard of good taste based on genuine understanding and appreciation of what is good about the thing.

After limitation comes the next principle, that of acceptance. In a world of infinitely varied human beings, there can be no equality of gifts. The child must be able to accept this inequality, to recognize and to respect the talents of others; and most of all he must learn to accept his own inadequacy, or paucity, of endowment. He must realize that no human being can do more than use to the full what he potentially has: but that he *can* do *that*. By such acceptance, the child will learn tolerance and will be free from at least some of the frustrations of life. Much of this can be learned in a classroom: but it can be learned best of all in group activities outside the timetable—the play, the orchestra or chamber-music group, the opera (in preparation and in performance), the school magazine, fairly large-scale projects of one sort or another that may or may not involve presentation to a 'public'. In such activities a number of individuals are concerned in diverse capacities; the contribution of each is important, but attention is focused primarily on the play, the symphony, the magazine, their self-interest becoming submerged in a corporate interest. Interpretative and creative group-activities of this kind teach the young to understand one another and to understand human nature as distinct from the nature only of material.

In all group activity, the accent should be on doing, rather than on the completed production or performance. The more the young learn to contrive and to improvise, to use their powers of imagination and ingenuity, and to see things through to the end 'until they be thoroughly finished,' the less likely will they be to accept everything 'on a plate.'

Moreover, children can discover that art and music are not only for a gifted few, but that they can be practised in public, or in private, by the many. It is important to choose plays, music, etc. that are good and worth doing, and also suitable in the widest sense, that is good of their kind rather than sophisticated: chosen in order to extend and deepen the child's experience, and not merely to pander to the producer's desire to have a shot at something out of the ordinary merely to startle, and to show how advanced the Dramatic Society is. Where learning by heart is necessary, the material should be intrinsically worth the effort. Here, too, by working on good material, the children begin to develop powers of discrimination. At least, they can be given a chance to like the best, and if they reject it—well, that's that. After all, educators are largely concerned with exposing children to the best influences they know, in the faith that the readiness to respond to the best is inherent in them, even if latent.

So to experience. The child must have opportunities to apply his own experience: those little bits and pieces of wisdom (about God, about people and about things) which he has gathered and which represent his experience of life. This he must now begin to use as the touchstone by which to test the vast welter of ideas, theories, values, admonitions which flood his mind from innumerable sources at this time, and from which he must fit together for himself something coherent and adequate. The emergence from secondhand beliefs proved by the experience of others into the formulation of his own first hand ones is a slow and stumbling process, which must begin during adolescence.

At first he may be tentative, confused, aggressive, defensive: it is difficult for him to extricate, from the values and opinions with which he has been imbued consciously or unconsciously at home, those he wants, as an independent individual, to feel he is accepting and making his own. He receives material through the written word and the spoken word: books, newspapers, grown-ups, the radio, discussions formal and informal in company with his fellows. By listening, by contributing his share, he must train himself to select, to test, to retain or discard, until some clear ideas and convictions about religion, politics, social affairs slowly begin to crystallize, and more than that, to make sense to him. It is vital that he should hear about these things from those who know: those with whom he can have some personal contact—people who are honest, and who believe and practise what they say.

Hence the great value and importance of a religious discussion group with staff and children present together, of the more serious type of debate, of world affairs talks by outside speakers and of private talks with teachers at school. In this connection, the responsibility and influence of the adult are immense. The young are quick to recognize integrity (and the reverse) and are naturally prone to look for and admire wisdom and insight in grown-ups. In practical affairs, teachers must be ready to share their skill, and skills, and the fruits of their experience, with the novices in their care: to give encouragement and informed criticism and to show that they expect things from them. They must be ready with a challenge.

The enthusiast whether inside or outside the classroom is probably the best kind of teacher, because he is caught up in his subject and is less liable to be possessive and to impose his own personality. To be of use he must know to some extent where he is going himself; he must have a philosophy of life which is reflected in the way he lives and acts. Whatever help adults are able to give, however, they cannot really *teach* a child what he needs. That he can only discover for himself.

The fact that we have said nothing about school games should not be taken to mean that we do not regard them as having an important place in school life—at the very least a high utilitarian value in the physical development of boys and girls. But far more than that: there is no doubt that many sorts of courage (and there are a thousand sorts), of enterprise and physical skill are developed by team games. Their direct value, however, in producing Christians has sometimes been exaggerated. It may be true that team games can develop to some degree the habit of recognizing the existence of other people and of understanding that some objectives can only be achieved by co-operation with them. They may provide the opportunity for the growth of wider loyalties so that a boy learns to think in terms of his House or his School and to put them before his own personal interests. It is true, nevertheless, that most frequently his own personal interests and those of the school coincide. He knows, for example, that if he plays an unselfish game he is more likely to remain in the team than if he plays a selfish one, and, without being unduly cynical, one may wonder how often a boy would be really glad to be dropped from the first team if he knew that he was being replaced by a better player who would thus improve the team's chance of success. The most that can be said for some games is that they teach self-control, and thus have a civilizing influence. The kind of 'unselfishness' which results from learning to co-operate with other members of a team is rather different from the dying to self which results from an encounter with the Cross, or even with one of the deeper parts of oneself.

CHAPTER TEN

The School and the Ordinary Child

THERE ARE plenty of ordinary children in grammar and in public schools as well as modern. For 'ordinariness' is not a matter of intelligence quotient alone, or of being drawn from a particular social class. By the term is meant, rather, boys and girls of sound but not outstanding intellectual ability, willing to follow a lead, desiring to be normal and for the most part quite ready to recognize that they are not high flyers. The large majority of ordinary children of between eleven and fifteen are of course in secondary modern schools or the 'modern' streams of bilateral or comprehensive schools. Two-thirds indeed of all English children between these ages are in such schools. But it would be wrong to exaggerate the difference either in social background or in general assumptions between many children in grammar schools—especialy those in C and D forms—and many in modern schools. The values and value-judgments of our civilization inhabit both groups. Grammar school education may once have been for a significant minority of the population who seized the opportunity because they wanted it or whose parents wanted it for them. Now it is given freely to all who pass the eleven-plus examination at the appropriate level.

As more and more children stay on at modern schools until sixteen or over, as a greater proportion of these schools are accommodated in good buildings and as more and more of their pupils find themselves not cut off from taking an external examination, the social recognition given to grammar and modern schools is likely to grow more nearly equal.

Though at present relatively few pupils from modern schools go to work far away from their own district, while many go from grammar schools to distant universities, colleges or jobs, even in this respect differences between the two types of school are tending to dwindle.

It is true that of the 3,500 secondary modern schools of the country too many are still housed 'downtown' in wretched buildings, and here there are sometimes problems not paralleled in schools of the same general character housed delightfully on a town's outskirts. 'To teach in a modern school in a poor area of an industrial city,' writes one correspondent, 'is to work on the frontier. The teacher is not cushioned by such bourgeois middle-class values as respect for authority, respect for property, respect for people as individuals. He finds himself confronted by, involved in, situations where the social and moral codes which operate are so different from his own that he feels an alien, almost an intruder. He is forced to realize that his way of life has little in common with that of the children he hopes to teach. On the frontier it is not possible for a teacher to maintain false illusions about human nature, either his own or that of others.' But if only a proportion of secondary modern schools are 'on the frontier' in this sense, most of them— like many grammar schools—are on the frontier in several others. The children generally come from homes which have much more money than a few years ago and in which material values are dominant. 'We have built up a tradition of co-operation in the school during the last few years,' a mistress reported, 'and the staff have no difficulty now in keeping people after school hours for some reason—rehearsals, making apparatus, etc. (often they go home first to do the shopping or "get father's tea" and then return), but if ever the question is asked—either directly or indirectly —whether *we* shall be paid 'overtime' their verdict is very definite; we are "soft".' Literacy is prized in many districts chiefly because it has a cash value, though since in these days literacy is no condition of employment at high wages it counts for less, especially in slum areas, than might at first be supposed. But a schoolmistress in a suburban school in a popular area of Middlesex still can write: 'The children are well turned out and the majority have television. School journeys to the continent are over-subscribed. . . . The children have for the most part accepted the values of their background. Money is the biggest inducement. They do not want responsibility or promotion. But the girls are keenly interested in planning and setting up a home that will last.'

This high rating of material possessions and 'good money' is, after all, not surprising in an age when a different hierarchy of values has lost its hold; and where men long for some protection against life and what it can do, however temporary and deliberate the forgetfulness. A flowing current of money underneath does give some sort of dancing stability to the floating twig; and 'keeping up with the Joneses' is a social relationship of a kind. This is one of the key maxims of our civilization, applying as much to Harley Street as to Paradise Row. Ordinary children educated in a society organized like ours have fewer encouragements than is sometimes imagined to regard themselves as in any real sense responsible for what goes on. Fortunes are not made by people like them—save maybe by a chance win in the pools. There is in fact comparatively little expectation of escape from one's social stratum, and not much wish for that, but also no longer a looking beyond the present life towards a more happy, full or just existence beyond the grave.

Yet ordinary children, all said and done, are as loving and as good at heart, as direct and full of energy as any; and this is certainly true of many who are below average in intelligence and quite unacademic in their interests. 'People are so steeped in success values,' writes a teacher of backward children, 'that even a Christian teacher finds difficulty in refraining from estimating an intelligent child more highly as a person than a dull one. Because they live in a world where personal success is highly important, Christian teachers inevitably over-value the importance of intelligence. It is easy to fall into the temptation of regarding high intelligence as attributable to the person who is intelligent and to forget that intelligence is itself a divine gift, the presence or absence of which should in no way alter the teacher's attitude to the child. Not that the teacher should despise intelligence, or any other aspect of human personality, but a respect for intelligence often goes with lack of respect for the less intelligent. There are teachers who are sentimental about the less intelligent and wish to disguise their limitations from them, depriving them in this way of the opportunity for self-knowledge and for adjustment to the reality of their own lack of ability. Sentimentality is as much to be avoided as either patronising benevolence or contempt, for it too springs from an identification of the person with certain personal attributes. No one should be pitied for lack of grace of body or swiftness of thought or any pre-eminent attractions or skill. We are as we are through no merit or demerit of ourselves; the presence or absence of any ability is irrelevant. But this is not to say that a slow learner is dispensed from using every ounce of energy in discovering his own peculiar potentialities and in fulfilling God's purpose by developing them.'

What can be done for the moral education of the ordinary and even the backward child? No teacher will get very far with his pupils, be they clever or dull, in this or any other matter, if he makes them feel at heart that they are failures. The good family and the good school are both places where no one feels he is of little worth. If intelligent boys and girls can be enabled to think their way through problems, those of lower mental ability can at least be helped to consider some of the pros and cons and to make a deliberate personal judgment after seeing more of the evidence than they had before. Relying much less upon the written word than with the more intellectual children, the teacher can through drama, stories, recounted incidents, art and films help children of quite moderate ability to imagine, consider and think about situations in which human, moral and religious problems are presented. B.B.C. and I.T.V. broadcasts yield much matter that challenges and can be discussed.

For many years now the B.B.C. has put on programmes designed to encourage children aged fourteen—fifteen to think about moral problems and to see if it is possible to help them to reason abstractly on why some actions are right and some wrong. The programmes consist in part of dramatised scenes. Some of these are invented from family and Youth Club situations (e.g. fair shares of the family income; a football captain deciding whether to drop his best friend from the team). Others are taken from books (e.g. *The Cruel Sea, Cry, the Beloved Country, Testament* by R. C. Hutchinson, etc.). It has been noticed that the children who listen to and discuss these programmes hardly ever tackle the question, 'Why is this action right or wrong?' When faced with it they rarely go beyond the answer, 'It wouldn't be fair,' 'It would be cruel,' or 'My Mum wouldn't like it.' Ethical questions in this form seem to be too abstract for them. If they are discussing a case of stealing, for example, such answers as 'It hurt someone else' or 'I would be ashamed to do it' do not occur to them. The idea that certain actions are anti-social or a betrayal of one's own standards rarely appear in these discussions.

The usual reaction to an ethical situation in which a decision has to be made is, 'Here is a mess, how do we get out of it?' Solutions are ingenious and often far-fetched. Rarely does a problem seem insoluble—there is always a compromise. For instance one dramatised illustration a few years ago was based upon the true story of a Czech boy whose father was killed by the Nazis and whose mother was taken to a concentration camp. The boy was brought up by excellent foster-parents and years later the mother, released from prison, found her son again. The American Army authorities had to decide whether the boy should continue with the foster-parents or go back to his mother. In one school the children produced the following solutions to this difficult problem. The mother and the foster-mother could live together; the boy could try his real mother for twelve months to see how he liked it; the boy could go to foster-parents and to the mother for alternate weeks. When a vote was taken twenty-five were for the real mother and eighteen for the foster-mother.

To very many children the greatest of all virtues is justice —or as they call it 'fair play'. On two occasions the parable of the Prodigal Son was used as an illustration. Comments from those who taught the children showed that, once the class was answering naturally and not merely saying what the teacher might appear to want them to say, the answer to the question 'Whose side are you on—the Prodigal Son's or the Elder Brother's?' was almost always 'The Elder Brother's.' The fact that the elder son was grumpy and unforgiving, narrow and unimaginative, appeared hardly to matter. The point was that he hadn't had fair play, and justice was so much more important than forgiveness. Indeed forgiveness seemed barely to have entered their own experience. Even if things went seriously wrong at home the storm would gradually die down and the whole affair would be pushed on one side within a week or so.

There is no remedy of course for such an absence of personal realization except a coming to realize. That is why developing sensibility and imagination is so important; and why stories and music—and personal suffering too—have a part to play. There can be no short cuts in giving education of the illuminating, inward, personal sort which really matters. Mere moral instruction skims only the surface; such teaching has to find an echo, has to touch an experience, a nerve ending, if it is to be felt and not to be taken simply as one more example of 'the stuff they tell you at school.'

In one of the B.B.C. programmes the reading of the parable from St. Luke's Gospel was preceded by a parallel modern story. In this a boy, Tom, imprisoned for theft, wrote to his parents asking if he could come home again when he was released. The parents gladly agreed but the daughter, Janet, rebelled against the idea. One B.B.C. Education Officer who heard this programme with a class of backward boys reported as follows:

'On scene three everybody was on the side of Tom, the boy who was coming out of prison. Janet was utterly unreasonable and most unfair. Yes, it would have been the same if it had been a girl who had been in prison and a boy who flew off the handle. I tried to make them see Janet's point of view. They remembered that she was afraid of what her friends would think—also her boy friend (but he had made little impact and most of the class forgot him)— and one boy said she might have lost her job. But still she got no sympathy. But in this they were inconsistent, for they had no sympathy to spare for the Prodigal Son of the Gospel. "He'd go and do it again." I found that the father's forgiveness implied in their minds that the prodigal would get a new allowance. They thought the brother's indignation was justified. Janet, therefore, was too deficient in forgiveness, but the prodigal's father forgave too easily.'

Most children are interested in ethical problems when posed in terms of simple and familiar situations, or as issues within an exciting story. But they tend to be pretty rigid and orthodox about what they think is right and wrong, however much they may fail in practice. They believe in honesty, telling the truth, being kind (especially to animals), and above all in fair play. In general they do approve of the common virtues. Yet the large majority of ordinary adolescents are not likely to do any great amount of fundamental thinking. Even in a lively discussion group on a vital issue the duller ones—and some of the others too—will need a good deal of guidance. That is quite compatible with a really personal involvement, however, if the guidance is done with sympathy. What they may most often need are actual examples of right and wrong actions, so that they will be able to recognize the right; and the best training is to present them with issues of right and wrong with some fairly explicit help towards seeing which is the right kind of solution and why it is the better.

A discussable, and common, situation is that of 'pinching' things from an employer. 'These girls believe that mother and father are entitled to "get things" from their places of employment. If the product of father's factory is something that is useful in school, one has the greatest difficulty in refusing to accept what one suspects is, in reality, "stolen property". This attitude is reflected in the girls' comments from time to time—if a girl volunteers to do some shopping for a teacher and if one of the required items is something that can be obtained from school stock—a reel of cotton for instance—the girl will often point out that there is no need to buy it. My experience, when I have pointed out that school property is not my property, has often been to receive a motherly, "But that doesn't matter!" as if from a worldly wise woman to an *ingénue*.' Why should it be in the least wrong to take advantage of such opportunities for free gifts? This is a question worth thrashing out in the classroom.

'I was asked in an informal discussion last January,' writes a schoolmaster, 'if I thought that it was right that the B.B.C. should bring so much religion into Christmas. I felt that the very way the class accepted this as a subject for discussion—rather in the sense that this thing "religion at Christmas" "has increased, is increasing, and ought to be diminished"—epitomised how deep was their ignorance of the Christian faith and how little we manage to make contact with the problem.'

Where the class teacher is interested and sees the possibilities of the subject, there is much to be said for his teaching scripture to his own form or class. And in scripture well taught abundant chances arise for just such discussions of moral problems as have been instanced. There is without doubt danger in making the subject too hard and too technical for the ordinary child. Many agreed syllabuses themselves tend to be over-ambitious. The Bible is much the most difficult and complex book used in any modern school and most grammar schools. The teacher who chose a history book of comparable difficulty of vocabulary and presentation would rightly be condemned, and few literary texts of a similar standard are likely to be used. Over and over again ordinary children are unable to paraphrase or explain well known passages in the Gospels. This is a powerful argument for a much greater use of modern translations. Even Rieu has his obscurities, but the response of the children to a text like his is sometimes remarkable. The proportion of ordinary children having links with a church varies greatly. A number will certainly get no scripture knowledge from anywhere but their day school. In some schools seventy-five per cent of children go to church regularly; in one in the south of England as few as six per cent appear to do so.

'I like going to church, I am in the choir and I am very lucky because my family do not laugh at me for going,' wrote a fourteen-year-old girl in Battersea in an essay about herself. Family approval and general social approval are likely to be even more influential with ordinary children than with those of marked individuality. David Riesman's penetrating study of the changing western character, *The Lonely Crowd*, contains an account of an interview with a twelve-year-old girl who had been reading some comics:

'I like Superman better than the others because they can't do everything Superman can do. Batman can't fly and that is very important.'

'Would you like to be able to fly?'

'I would like to be able to fly if everybody else did, but otherwise it would be kind of conspicuous.'

Most children and most grown-ups do not like to be 'kind of conspicuous'. They will tend to do, according to their ability, more or less what everybody else does. Hence the power of the group whether in school or, later on, in factory. If the school is going to prepare its children for the real world it must not get too far from contemporary concerns and the sort of everyday life into which they will presently be going.

The grammar school will send at least a fair proportion of its A and B stream boys into a professional life, where competition is dominant and promotion still depends for many on the qualifications they can amass, on their ability to prove that they deserve a higher status and a better salary than the next man. But any school can easily overwork competitive motives and underestimate the importance of helping children to keep in good and close relationship with each other on the job and the importance of the preservation of such relationships. The large majority of those going out at any rate from the C and D streams of modern schools will be earning as big a wage at twenty-five as they will at fifty, apart of course from any annual increases which their Trades Union may get—for all alike—year by year. Their world is not going to put much premium on competition after they leave school; it is going to put a great deal on co-operation.

The good group is one which binds its members together in an outgoing enterprise or a deep experience that is worthwhile for all who take part in it. The best sort of co-operation is a product of shared responsibility. The schools most likely to be successful in giving Christian education for a changing world are those which manage to put some responsibility upon the children for the temper of the whole. Within a dozen years the modern school may well be keeping sixty per cent of its pupils to the age of sixteen, and twenty per cent to the age of seventeen. One of the efforts must be to devolve more real responsibility upon potential leaders among the children themselves: to try to treat as many children as possible as if they were a bit older rather than a bit younger than they are. A young factory worker said not long ago: 'They treat you like kids at school; at jobs we have to act grown-up. It comes as a shock.' The shock is much lessened already in schools where the boys and girls feel that upon their sense and judgment and friendliness almost everything really depends. Many children of no remarkable intellectual ability can take far more responsibility than they are given at school and will learn more poise and more unselfishness from taking it.

CHAPTER ELEVEN

Conclusion

ONE OF our main contentions in this book has been that Christian education is not only, perhaps not even chiefly, a matter of teaching religious knowledge or the text of the Bible. The way in which science, literature, history, are taught has a great and unavoidable bearing on our pupils' understanding of things. What we are maintaining, in other words, is that education through any subject must take place inside another more capacious kind of education, which is both liberal and religious. To put a scientific or literary education inside a Christian framework is to do in the life and upbringing of the individual what history has been doing for a thousand years in the life and growth of western society. In the same way, education in objectivity has to take place inside an education which involves deep personal interest and concern. Without a belief in the worthwhileness of life, what is the use of objectivity? Of what service is freedom if one has no convictions, no beliefs and no will to live in the spirit? There is nothing irrational about commitment; it is permanent non-commitment that seeks to trade out of human life and the nature of things.

Schools differ greatly in the sheer power of the education they give. To teach a subject so that it has consequences to the general outlook and orientation of those who learn it will be much easier in some schools than others. Much will, of course, depend on the individual teacher; but in the long run an immense amount depends upon the school itself. What can be taught in one place by a pretty ordinary teacher cannot be got over at all in another except by a genius. The greatest force a school has for keeping its children stable yet open-minded too is its own group-spirit. The individual child catches his values from the age and nation he belongs to, and more particularly from the groups within that age and nation to which he feels he specially belongs: his family, his friends and his school. The more he really feels he belongs to his school the more power it has over him and within him.

Schools, as we have suggested, tend to be better at 'covering the ground' in a subject and at securing concentration and 'accusative' attention than at educating also a more relaxed, untense awareness. If Christian education is to be given, a waiting and receptive mind from time to time is indispensable. A school whose discipline is right will be one which is securing a high potential of energy in its children and at the same time allowing it to have fairly free expression. The direction in which it expresses itself will, however, be influenced by the school's own sense of direction. It is the principles for which a teacher stands, partly as a representative of the school, partly as a person, that are the true source of his authority. These may be conscious or unconscious, but if he has no perceptions and no principles, he has no real authority, though he may deceive some of his pupils into thinking that he has. Part of his task is to help them to learn freely to recognize power and real authority when they see them; though moments of such perception involve a high degree of self-discipline. On the other hand, any compelled recognition of authority tends to destroy sensitiveness, and free recognition becomes less and less possible the more often compulsion is used. The Christian method basically is one of saying 'Here is the truth, but you as an individual must choose whether or not you will accept it.' The school must not, even if it could, dictate what people shall believe: but at the same time it must treat them as capable of belief and able at moments to live at the levels faith demands. The teacher who does not see his pupils as people with immortal souls has no right to think that he has one himself.

Whatever the school can do, however, the world of work into which most of the children will be going will be both a continuation of their education and a test of what has been given. If they have not begun to grow a core by the age of fifteen or sixteen it may be very difficult for most of them to grow one afterwards. Going to work is of course in itself a necessary part of moral education. For one thing, in factory or workshop or office, the young are faced with the inescapable necessity of carrying through a particular job. This is part of the process of growing up. They have to stick to one task for a period and to some extent to commit themselves to it. To do this is one of the secrets of personal development. It helps to bring to an end the period of prolonged play, that is, of irresponsible activity, characteristic of childhood. The time comes when the only way of being responsive is to accept responsibility. Mere conformity is not enough: there is a whole gulf between it and making genuinely moral decisions.

Many boys and girls passing from school to industry suffer a shock at the different moral standards prevalent at the work bench, and at what one boy called the 'malicious selfishness' which is on the whole so alien to the school world, so common outside it. If proof of this were needed it is to be found in the armour of 'hard boiledness' which young people put on within three months of taking up their job in the world. There is room for many closer links between schools and factories, notably through more frequent contacts between teachers and the welfare officers of firms in the school's area. There is scope for discussion groups which bring together people in their last year at school and people already at work. What is so often forgotten is that those who leave school for work at fifteen are doing so before the age when friends are for the most part made. In the factory or the workshop it is difficult to make friends in the same sense or at the same depth as in college or university. The accusations brought against many young people working in factories in their teens are that they lack 'stickability' and zest. It is forgotten that they are no older than sixth formers or undergraduates, who are expected to sample a great variety of experiences, to have many temporary enthusiasms, which the greater part of the population is given little opportunity or encouragement to pursue. Safety in all these matters lies in the possession by the individual of a 'still point,' a believing centre, a philosophy of life which can grow. When county colleges come into being it is extraordinarily important that their bias should not be merely technical, but that they should be places where thought can be challenged about the meaning of work, relations with other people, the right use of money and time and the real purpose of living.

It is clear enough that one of the main needs if children are to be educated with a Christian outlook is a supply of teachers of many subjects other than religious knowledge, as well as divinity itself, who understand the importance of their own presuppositions. This is a problem for Christians on training college staffs and for those in universities who have to do with the educating of teachers. One difficulty of some size is that of keeping teacher-trainers vital themselves. They must not only be alive when they join a staff but they must stay alive. However good their scholarship, they must keep in touch with the changing temper of the sixth forms from which their students come, and that of contemporary life. They must see that inevitably the teachers they train are going to be censors and judges and filters of what children learn; and that this is part of being their brothers' keepers. But perhaps the most important thing of all is to secure that the teachers who are trained should show to their children both their convictions and their understanding and not be afraid of doing it. There is little room in the teaching profession either for those who do not know what they believe or for those unable to show love.

Even Christians often lack conviction today that the education given to children—at any rate in schools—has any overriding purpose. Rather they think of it as having only a considerable variety of diverse, separable purposes. Yet it is important for all of us to be

'studious more to see
Great Truths, than touch and handle little ones',

for always, even in matters of knowledge, 'in order to *have* effectively, it is necessary to *be* in some degree'. No doubt Christian education has to do with *being*, but learning to be in this sense starts by learning to look and feel and apprehend in ways found to be particularly full of meaning by past generations of Christians, stretching back to Christ himself. In other words, what is involved is learning a tradition—a tradition of seeing and understanding. A tradition is a heritage and as Kitson Clark has said, 'perhaps the most important thing to remember about a heritage is that it may be lost'. The personal needs of ordinary boys and girls in 1960, however fast the world is changing, are not greatly different from the needs of those whom Christ knew. Man may be modern but he is ancient too; he may seem to belong to the present but the past is still inside him; the present is only as it were that part of the past now on the surface. And man can escape from his deeper self only at the cost of barrenness.

The outlook and achievements of children without doubt

depend to a remarkable extent on the expectations which adults have of them. But no tradition in an age so full of question about accepted habits and expectations as ours can any longer continue to function safely in unconsciousness. If we go on assuming that the education of a Christian outlook is implicit in the life of a school, because it has a chapel, or a period of opening worship every day, or because religious knowledge according to a good agreed syllabus still appears on the timetable, we may soon find it missing altogether. We need to become more conscious of some of these powerful presuppositions alien to a Christian understanding of things—and therefore in turn to Christian conduct—which are embodied in our teaching of this subject and that, and, in a hundred almost unnoticeable ways, in what we do and say as teachers and as men and women.

APPENDIX I

Members of the Institute of Christian Education's Study and Research Committee

Mr. D. G. O. AYERST, H.M.I.

Mr. A. R. BIELBY, Headmaster, Huddersfield New College, Huddersfield, Yorks.

Miss E. A. BLACKBURN, Headmistress, Walthamstow Hall, Kent

Mr. E. L. BRADBY, Principal, St. Paul's College, Cheltenham

Professor C. A. COULSON, Rouse Ball Professor of Applied Mathematics, University of Oxford

Miss JOAN M. DAVIS, Lecturer, University of London Institute of Education

Professor M. V. C. JEFFREYS, Professor of Education, University of Birmingham

Lady OGILVIE, Principal, St. Anne's College, Oxford

Dr. R. PERRY, Headmaster, Hengrove Comprehensive School, Bristol

Dr. MARJORIE REEVES, Vice-Principal, St. Anne's College, Oxford

Dr. J. W. D. SMITH, Principal Lecturer in Religious Education, Jordanhill Training Centre, Glasgow

Miss J. E. SLADDEN, Secretary, Institute of Christian Education, London

The Right Rev. R. W. STOPFORD, Lord Bishop of Peterborough

Dr. L. J. STROUD, Headmaster, King Edward VI School, Southampton

Rev. R. C. WALTON, Producer of Religious Programmes, School Broadcasting Department, B.B.C.

Mr. G. N. WHITFIELD, Headmaster, Hampton Grammar School, Middlesex

Mr. R. E. WILLIAMS, H.M.I.

Miss J. WRIGHT, Headmistress, Lyndon Girls' School, Solihull, Warwickshire.

Mr. ROGER YOUNG, Headmaster, George Watson's School for Boys, Edinburgh

Mr. T. J. P. YORK, Headmaster, Merchant Taylors' School, Liverpool

Professor W. R. NIBLETT, Professor of Education, University of London (*Chairman*)

Dr. BASIL YEAXLEE, Sometime Reader in Educational Psychology, University of Oxford (*Vice-Chairman*)

APPENDIX II

Among those who submitted memoranda or contributed material used by the Committee in its deliberations were the following :

J. A. ANKERSON, Headmaster, Hackney Free Secondary School, London, E.9

W. H. BACKHOUSE, Headmaster, Parlington County School, Aberford, Yorkshire

Mrs. K. BICKERDIKE, Assistant Mistress, Queen Anne Grammar School for Girls, York

J. A. BOLTON, Assistant Master, King Edward's School for Boys, Birmingham, 15

British Council of Churches Education Discussion Group

Miss C. W. CLARK, Advisory Secretary, Institute of Christian Education

KENNETH A. CROFTS, Headmaster, Liverpool Collegiate School

Rev. R. E. DAVIES, formerly Chaplain, Kingswood School, Bath

Rev. JOHN DREWETT, Rector, St. Mary's, Lothbury, E.C.2

W. E. KENNETH FORD, Senior Science Master, Heckmondwike Grammar School

D. A. FRITH, Headmaster, Archbishop Holgate's Grammar School, York

Miss C. B. GALTON, Headmistress, Cranborne Chase School, Crichel, Dorset

Dr. MARJORIE GRENE, Senior Research Fellow, University of Leeds Institute of Education

Dr. V. Grubb, Principal, Salisbury Training College

P. Hammond, Assistant Master, Romford Secondary Modern School, Essex

Miss Ena Harper, Assistant Mistress, Molesey Boys' Modern School, Surrey

Norman Hillas, Senior History Master, Cockburn High School, Leeds

Miss F. Humphrey-Edwards, Headmistress, Cale Green High School, Stockport

J. O. P. Jones, Headmaster, Longlevens Secondary Modern School, Gloucester

Dr. A. G. Joselin, Deputy Director, Institute of Education, The University, Leicester

Rev. R. G. Lunt, Headmaster, King Edward's School for Boys, Birmingham, 15

Rev. Dr. John Marsh, Principal, Mansfield College, Oxford

Mr. J. Melser, Lecturer in English, Ardmore College, New Zealand

Miss M. Miles, Headmistress, Mayfield School, Putney, S.W.15

Rev. J. W. Packer, Headmaster, Canon Slade School, Bolton

Miss R. Pearse, Headmistress, Mary Datchelor School, London, S.E.5

Miss C. Phillips, Assistant Mistress, Worcester City Grammar School for Girls

F. B. Pinion, Headmaster, Woodhouse Grammar School, near Sheffield

John Prickett, Headmaster, Kent College, Canterbury

Rev. Ronald Rees, Overseas Secretary, Institute of Christian Education

L. Arnaud Reid, Professor of the Philosophy of Education, University of London

Miss Seonaid Robertson, Senior Lecturer in Art and Crafts, Doncaster Training College

Rev. E. C. D. Stanford, Educational Secretary, British Council of Churches

Miss MURIEL TELFORD, Headmistress, Leek High School for Girls, Staffordshire

T. E. A. VERITY, Lecturer, Manchester College of Technology

WILLIAM WALSH, Professor of Education, University of Leeds

Miss A. J. WHITAKER, Lecturer, Stockwell Training College, Bromley, Kent

C. B. WHYATT, Assistant Master, Cambridge Road Secondary Modern School, Cheshunt

Miss VIOLET WILKINSON, Tutor, Oxford University Department of Education

Miss M. M. WINGATE, Principal, Balls Park Training College, Hertford

WYNDHAM WOODWARD, Headmaster, Spalding Grammar School, Lincolnshire

FOUNDRY PRESS, LTD., BRERETON ROAD, BEDFORD